AF251138

Dream Factory on The Nile

Pierre Sioufi Collection
of
Egyptian Cinema Lobby Cards

Introduction: Rasha Azab
Photographic reproduction: Dominique Mauri
Translation assistance: Karaz Hamdy – Mohamed Moftah
Compiled and edited by Sherif Boraïe

First published in 2019 by Zeitouna
30 Abdine Square, Cairo, Egypt
admin@zeitouna.com

Dar el-Kutub nº 20117/2019
ISBN 978 977 5864 30 7

Printed in Egypt

DREAM FACTORY ON THE NILE

PIERRE SIOUFI COLLECTION
OF
EGYPTIAN CINEMA LOBBY CARDS

ZEITOUNA

For Pierre

1961–2018

Avant-Propos

The Pierre Sioufi Cinema Collection includes over 10,000 lobby cards from over 1,300 films. The extensive collection also includes thousands of Egyptian, American, European, Soviet, Turkish, Indian, and Chinese film posters and lobby cards, as well as Arabic posters of foreign films.

Lobby cards are an excellent tool to study the history of cinema. Considered by some an art form, lobby cards attract collectors for their compact size, their original still photographs of film stars, the creative artwork around the stills, and the artists who designed them.

In Egypt, the lobby card, more than the poster, almost invariably gave a longer credit list that included the production company, cast and crew, director, screenwriter, and music composer. The earliest seen lobby cards in Egypt today date back to 1930.

Lobby cards were placed in the lobby or foyer of a cinema, sometimes hung in elaborate frames or displayed on an easel near the box office. They were sent by film production companies to theater owners in sets of eight to twenty images to lure the public into the theater.

As the film industry progressed, lobby cards became more creative and sophisticated. The artwork, sometimes lettered and colored by hand, reflected the poster. A graphic design industry grew around the production of lobby cards, posters, and publicity paraphernelia.

The production of lobby cards in Egypt continued until 2009/2010, although it changed from stills mounted on cardboard to offset-printed paper.

On the Egyptian Cinema Industry (1896–1997)

Rasha Azab

Genesis (1896–1919)

Bright lights and paved streets, the city of Alexandria shimmered on the Mediterranean. The Manshiya district was the first to install electrical street lamps. Big hotels and cafés soon followed. The bright yellow electric tramway cut across the *afrangi* (foreign) quarters, attracting more spectators than passengers, its pricey ticket beyond the means of the average Alexandrian.

These were the last days of the nineteenth century. Alexandria had become Egypt's second capital. Viceroy Mohamed Ali Pasha had restored life to the coastal city by digging the Mahmoudieh Canal that brought Nile water and rejuvenated the economy. A railway line connected it to Cairo in 1856. Alexandria and its port became the destination of Greek, Italian, French, Armenian, and Levantine merchants. Foreign consulates congregated in the city around their communities, adding European color to its character.

Rising from the ruins of British bombardment in 1882, the city restored its ancient cosmopolitanism. The wealthy foreign community lived in Ramleh, Manshiya, Muharram Bey, and Tewfikieh. Their less affluent peers lived in the new districts of Ibrahimiya and Shatby. Egyptians, Moroccans, and some Levantines lived in the Turkish Quarter by the old eastern harbor.

From the city's foreign language newspapers, we learn of the first film screening in Egypt on November 5, 1896. The French *La Reforme* reported on the cinematographic equipment at the Tousson Exchange, where an Italian impresario, Henri Dello Strologo, held the first projection for an audience of Alexandria's high society. After initially pricing tickets at the considerable sum of four piasters, Dello Strologo slashed prices by half to attract more customers. Produced by the Lumière Brothers, the films featured the Opera Square in Paris, workers leaving their factory, and scenes of daily life in Europe.

After the successful Alexandria screenings, Dello Strologo forayed into Cairo with his projector and film reels. For days, the press speculated about the new invention arriving soon at Schneiden Hall in the Prince Halim Pasha estate in Ezbekia, the arts and social hub of the city. Dello Strologo invited the city's glitterati and held a special showing for Khedive Abbas Helmi II and his family at Kobba Palace.

Two months after his first screening, Dello Strologo rented a hall located between Tousson Exchange and Al-Hambra Theatre on Moharrram Bey Street in Alexandria. Cinematographe Lumière was soon followed by another in Cairo.

The successful screenings prompted Lumière to dispatch a representative in 1897 with new films to boost Dello Strologo's repertory and shoot films in Egypt. Thirty-five films were shot between Cairo and Alexandria, including the arrival of the train at the Ramleh Station, the Mahmal Procession, Citadel Square, Nahaseen Street, and traffic across Cairo's Kasr el-Nil Bridge. The

Lumière Brothers offered a franchise providing a projector and film reels for free in exchange for half the revenues.

The following year, a cinematographic projection took place in Port Said at the Eastern Exchange Hotel. The Edison company followed with a projection in 1899 at the Eden Theater in Alexandria.

The competition between Lumière and Edison to export equipment and films to Egypt ensured a proliferation of cinematographic projections that accompanied theatrical and music hall performances at the start of the twentieth century. Any café, music hall, or theater with ample space capitalized on the new business.

Edison sent a film crew in 1903 to shoot scenes in Egypt. In 1906, Urbanora opened in Alexandria, a cinematograph catering to the large Italian community.

Not to be outdone, Lumière dispatched another team to shoot footage in Egypt, the Levant, the Sudan, and Palestine. Their agents this time were Aziz Bendarli and Umberto Dorés, two partners who added cinematography to their photographic studio. They opened Cinephone Aziz and Dorés in 1906 (later renamed Cinema Belle Vue) where they presented their film *The Visit of Khedive Abbas Helmi II to the Scientific Institute of the Sidi Aboul Abbas Mosque* in 1907, considered to be the first local film. However, the Alexandrian newspaper *El-Baseer* cited the 1905 inauguration of Cinematograph Pathé, by Frenchman L. de Lagarenne with a reel featuring scenes of the Alexandria Cotton Exchange and the port during the arrival of the European post.

The Italian Dorés was well liked by Khedive Abbas Helmi and his entourage. When Prince Ahmed Fuad became Sultan of Egypt, Dorés was appointed his personal photographer. His apprentice at the time was a young Alexandria-born Italian, Alvise Orfanelli, whose film career spanned Egyptian cinema until the 1960s.

Between 1907 and 1917, newsreels and documentaries accompanied foreign films. In both Cairo and Alexandria, second- and third-class cinema halls appeared in poorer neighborhoods where features were shown after their rounds of first-class cinemas. Cinema halls spread to the provinces in Assiut, Mansoura, Suez, and Ismailia.

Egypt's audience devoured the offerings and clamored for more, as did foreign communities who watched their nations' films on Alexandria's screens. The city had become a vast hospital for Allied casualties of the Great War. The silver screen was a haven for all.

In 1917, the Banco di Roma branch in Alexandria, backed by Dorés and other Italian filmmakers, founded SITCIA, Egypt's first production company. It set up the first studio for film development and editing in Nozha and produced the first three feature films: *Deadly Flowers*, *The Bedouin's Honor*, and *Towards the Abyss*. All three films failed and the company lost its LE 20,000 capital. With a war-weary Italy and Banco di Roma in dire straits, SITCIA was liquidated.

Orfanelli bought the bankrupt company's equipment and launched his long cinematic career. In 1919, he opened his own studio in Alexandria equipped with a developing laboratory.

Until then, Cairo had no involvement in production. Joseph Mosseiri, of the wealthy Jewish-Italian Mosseiri family in Cairo, had established in 1915 Josy Film that owned a chain of cinema halls in Cairo, Alexandria, Port Said, and Suez, and that remained a prominent film distributer in Egypt until the 1950s.

Other attempts included the popular Egyptian Club Cinema in the Hussein district of Cairo that was installed by Abdel Rahman Salhein in the basement of his hotel.

Egypt's 1917 Almanac documented 36 cinema theaters, in addition to another 15 theaters mentioned in the local press in a list compiled by Mahmoud Ali in his book *The Dawn of Egyptian Cinema*, bringing the total to over 50.

Cairo's thriving theater scene had led a cultural renaissance and relief from the exhausting effects of the Great War. Audiences flocked to theaters with feverish enthusiasm. Performances by Sheikh Salama Hegazy, George Abyad, Naguib el-Rihani, Mounira el-Mahdiya, and Sayed Darwich played to full houses, the *Express* newspaper reported in February 1918.

After the Great War, Egypt's renaissance embraced the role of women, constitutional democracy, and civil rights. The new Egyptian university heralded an improved educational system after four decades of British Occupation. A national identity was on the rise, inspired by the 1919 Revolution whose ramifications persisted for years.

Formation (1920–1930)

Egyptians sought to learn the new art of cinema from two sources: the study of cinema in Europe and collaboration with foreigners and Egyptianized residents. Two of Egyptian cinema's pioneers were Alexandrian Mohamed Bayoumi, who traveled to Germany to became the first Egyptian to study cinema; and Mohamed Karim, Egypt's first actor, who had worked with SITCIA.

Ahmed el-Hadary said in his *Encyclopedia of Cinema* in Egypt that foreign filmmakers in Alexandria realized that a film's success depended on casting local actors loved by Egyptian audiences while they remain behind the camera.

Famous theater actors were cast for the first short movies: *Madame Loretta* (1919), filmed by Orfanelli, starring Fawzi el-Gazaerli and his Alexandrian troupe, followed by *The American Aunt* (1920), featuring comedy stage star Ali el-Kassar.

In 1923, Mohamed Bayoumi became the first Egyptian cinematographer to film a full-length feature film, *In the Land of Tutankhamun*, produced and directed by resident Italian lawyer Victor Rossito.

Bayoumi also produced *Amun* that recorded the return of Saad Zaghloul Pasha from exile. *Amun* was the first Egyptian-produced newsreel created in Bayoumi's studio, also the first founded by an Egyptian. The same year, he directed *Barsoum Seeks Employment*, the first short film shot, developed, and directed by an Egyptian.

Bayoumi then contacted the prominent industrialist Talaat Harb Pasha to impress the need for an Egyptian film company. By contributing his German equipment, Misr Acting & Film Company was born, the seed for Studio Misr ten years later.

Upon his return from art studies in Italy in 1921, Yousef Wahbi deplored the state of Egyptian theater and dismissed most productions as "comic burlesque." He founded Ramses Theater with his inheritance money, where he presented Shakespeare and Ibsen and where he enforced strict rules on actors to stick to the script, shouted at unruly audiences, and prohibited smoking in the auditorium. His troupe introduced new faces like Amina Rizk, Anwar Wagdi, and the rising star Aziza Amir.

Aziza Amir entered the world of cinema with a swooping adventure. After delays, difficulties and a slander campaign, *Laila* (1927) appeared—the first Egyptian business venture in cinema. With cinematography by Tullio Chiarini of SITCIA, it was initially directed by Turkish parvenu Wedad Orfy, and completed by Egypt-born Stephan Rosti. It was screened in first-class theaters which had until then only shown foreign-made films.

The female adventure was a success. Talaat Harb Pasha hailed Aziza Amir's work, telling her at the film's premiere that she succeeded where men had failed.

At the same time, the brothers Ibrahim and Badr Lama, Palestinian-born immigrants from South America, arrived in Alexandria, where they based their cinema enterprise. Their first production was *A Kiss in the Desert* (1927), a Rudolph Valentino–style film. Audiences and critics favored *Laila*. Unhindered, they founded Condor Film, aided by Orfanelli.

Orfanelli, who had separated from Dorés, chose a young Egyptian, Abdel Halim Nasr, and instructed him in filming and developing. *Laila* inspired several theater actresses. Amina Rizk played her first film, *Soad the Gypsy* (1928). Well-known Fatma Rouchdy presented her first film, *Disaster at the Pyramids* (1928), with the Lama Brothers.

Assia arrived from the Levant taking direct aim at cinema. She started as an actress and producer, assisted by her niece, Mary Queeny, who learned editing in addition to being an actress. She lured the young journalist Ahmed Galal to write scripts, then direct. A cinema trio was born.

Young filmmakers managed Misr Acting & Film Company, which specialized in documentary newsreels of Banque Misr and its affiliates. Mohamed Karim, who had returned from Italy, directed a few. In 1928, he attempted, unsuccessfully, to convince Talaat Harb Pasha to produce a full-length feature.

Karim turned to his boyhood friend, Yousef Wahbi, who had returned to theater to recover from a scathing attack on his proposed portrayal of Prophet Mohamed in film. After persuading Wahbi to produce a film without appearing in it, Karim resigned from Misr Company. Wahbi built Studio Ramses, Cairo's first, on a family plot in Imbaba for the interior scenes. The release of *Zeinab* (1930) was a success for both friends.

Diffusion (1931–1940)

Togo Mizrahi, a wildcard filmmaker in Alexandria, acquired Cinema Bacos and converted it into a studio for his first film, *The Abyss* (1930).

Egypt now had five studios: in Alexandria, Studio Alvise Orfanelli, the Lama Brothers' Condor Film, Mizrahi's Studio Bacos, and in Cairo, Wahbi's Studio Ramses, and Aziza Amir's Studio Heliopolis.

In 1931, the first talkie was screened in Cinema Al-Hambra in Alexandria. Cairo's audience heard Yousef Wahbi's voice in the first promotional reel about his upcoming movie, *The Upper Class*, a talkie based on his hit play of the same name.

Film companies competed to present the first talking film. Wahbi and Karim emerged victorious with their runaway success, *The Upper Class*, released in 1933. It was screened for four weeks running in Cairo, Alexandria, and Port Said simultaneously. It was a turning point in the industry, which had until then functioned with one single film copy shared among various movie theaters.

A month later, the musical film made its debut with *Song of the Heart*, produced by Nahas and Selections Behna in Alexandria. Behna became Egypt's first distribution company and *Song of the Heart* the first Egyptian film exported to Arab countries.

Song of the Heart ushered in the era of the Egyptian musical. It encouraged Mohamed Abdel Wahab to make his first film, *The White Rose* (1933). He drew Mohamed Karim away from Yousef Wahbi. They traveled to Paris to shoot the speaking sequences where the first Egyptian talkies were made. Abdel Wahab chose to record the songs in Berlin to ensure quality recordings of his voice.

The White Rose was a phenomenal leap both for the box office and the musical film—seventeen copies of the film were made with four screenings per day. Flush with success, the popular singer set up his own company, Abdel Wahab Films, presenting two of his films in the 1930s.

Also in 1933, Hungarian sound engineer Ladislav Szabo, who started in Orfanelli's Alexandria studio in Alexandria and was later known as Mohsen Szabo, manufactured a local sound recording machine. He established the Egyptian Talking Film Company, recording sound for Assia and Togo Mizrahi films.

After a hesitant beginning, momentum gathered. Assia produced one or two films a year, as did the Lama Brothers, whose bedouin films of Egypt as a desert with camels were contentious. Yousef Wahbi debuted as a film director after his separation from Karim, drawing on members of his theater troupe. And Togo Mizrahi rocketed with two or three popular comedy films a year.

Mizrahi developed a Hollywood-studio monopoly-like model, and upgraded Studio Bacos, where fourteen of his films were shot. He worked closely with Studio Alvise, whose laboratory now developed talkies. He used Abdel Halim Nasr, Orfanelli's protégé, as his cinematographer for all his films in the 1930s.

He signed talent for two or three films upfront: Fawzi el-Gazaerli, Ali el-Kassar, Taheya Carioca, Shalom, and his most important discovery, Laila Mourad. She had sung without appearing in *The Victims* (1935), then co-starred opposite Mohamed Abdel Wahab in *Long Live Love* (1938). By 1939, she became the star of a series of films bearing her name under exclusive contract to Mizrahi.

Cinema theaters were controlled by Egyptian Jews and foreigners—Mosseiri, Spiro Raissi, and the Politi Brothers. In 1931, Commerce School graduates founded the Egyptian Cinematograph Company, which folded after a year. In 1933, Cinema Fuad, under Egyptian management, approached Abdel Wahab to screen *The White Rose*, but he had committed to Raissi of Cinema Ideal. Nationalist students launched a public protest against Abdel Wahab and his film, successfully winning Cinema Fuad the rights to the second screening.

During the formative period, mansions of the upper class were used as sets for filming, influenced by the Italian Telefoni Bianchi movies that portrayed the elite's lifestyle. *When a Woman Loves* (1933), produced by Assia and directed by Ahmed Galal, was filmed in Saray Lotfallah. Another Assia film, *Shagaret el-Dor* (1935), was shot in the Heliopolis Hotel, now the Presidential Palace. *The White Rose*'s interior shots were filmed in the Naguib Yousef villa in Giza.

As the industry developed, studios proliferated. Studio Katsaros in downtown Cairo was created in a hall adjoining a furniture showroom to facilitate set preparation. Studio Nasibian was founded in Daher, a popular cinema district and a hub of the Egyptian Jewish community.

Studio Misr was inaugurated in 1935, ten years after Misr Acting & Film Company was established. It was the cumulative result of Banque Misr's growth, amid a drive to nationalize the economy, calls for independence that led to the 1936 Anglo-Egyptian Treaty followed by a partial British evacuation from Cairo, and the abrogation of the Capitulations.

Studio Misr ushered in a new level of production with multiple sets, modern film labs, and interior design workshops in a single location. The studio sent a batch of young filmmakers to study abroad and hired foreign experts in all departments. They honed a new generation of filmmakers who eventually took over when the foreigners were repatriated following the 1956 Suez War.

Studio Misr launched its first season in 1936 with *Wedad*, Umm Kalthum's first silver screen appearance and Egypt's largest production to date. The unprecedented LE 5,000 fee commanded by the diva was the equivalent of two Mizrahi productions.

The studio banked on its young talent. Niazi Mustafa directed *Salama Is Well* (1937) featuring theater comedy star Naguib el-Rihani, whose foray into film had hitherto been unlucky. Ahmed Badrakhan, returning from France, made his first film, *Something Out of Nothing* (1938) prompting Umm Kalthum to choose him as her favorite director. The 1930s concluded with a breakthrough movie, *Determination* (1939), directed by Kamal Selim, where the first Egyptian alley on set, designed by Wali-Eddine Sameh, ushered the beginning of Realism.

Despite the success and scope of its projects, Studio Misr suffered financial losses until the 1940s. A French expert was brought in, and a new policy of reducing production and renting out equipment and facilities to other companies paid off.

As war approached Alexandria in the late 1930s, the role of the city that had introduced film production in Egypt ended. Mizrahi and the Lama Brothers relocated to Cairo, where they established new studios. Orfanelli closed his studio because the building was in danger of collapsing.

During 1930s, 96 films were produced, led by Alexandrians: 15 by Mizrahi, 11 by the Lama Brothers, and 7 by Orfanelli.

Major Productions (1941–1952)

World War II raged. Film production relied on imported equipment and supplies. The black market ruled. The Egyptian government interceded with British Occupation authorities, and the Social Affairs Department became responsible for importing and distributing raw film. Prices were astronomical but war profiteers had accumulated capital; thus began the age of major cinema production in Egypt.

The war had disrupted global traffic, choking the supply of European films to the Middle East and increasing the control of American movies over local cinema theaters. Egyptian films penetrated Arab markets that had previously welcomed the gramophone records of Abdel Wahab and Umm Kalthum. Music had paved the way for Egyptian films. The local market covered 55% of production costs, while the Levant and Iraq accounted for 39%.

The Nile Film Company of the Talhami Brothers embarked on its first production, *The Victory of Youth* (1941), forerunner of a new genre of musical films that dominated the decade. It was the debut appearance of Farid el-Atrash and his sister Asmahan. Director Ahmed Badrakhan succeeded in the new genre, independent of Studio Misr and the voice of Umm Kalthum. (Note: a musical has two connotations in Arabic—*film ghenaii*, romantic singing film; and *film iste'radi*, the new genre spectacle film—although every film had its token dance.)

An earlier film in the new genre, *La Reine du Music Hall* (1936), produced by and starring the legendary Badia Masabni, had failed. But many of Masabni's music hall protégés like Farid el-Atrash, Taheya Carioca, Samia Gamal, Mohamed Fawzi, Ismail Yassin, and Naima Akef claimed fame and fortune for years to come.

The new musical, born of the theater and the music hall, was the refuge for World War II audiences. With the success of *The Victory of Youth* and an invigorated market, musical operetta films became a favorite investment for war profiteers.

Of the 400 movies produced between 1945 and 1952, 195 were musicals and 227 featured male and female singers in starring roles.

Two directors were at the heart of the new wave: Hussein Fawzi and Abbas Kamel, brothers of pioneer filmmaker Ahmed Galal. Fawzi began his career with Aziza Amir, followed by rising belly-dancing star Taheya Carioca, then his prize discovery, dancer Naima Akef. Kamel first worked with icons Ismail Yassin and Shekouko, discovered singing star Abdel Aziz Mahmoud, and went on to make action musicals.

Musical composition flourished. Abdel Wahab, Riyad el-Sonbati, and Zakaria Ahmed composed *tarab* (classical Arabic music); Farid el-Atrash the operetta; Ezzat el-Gaheli, Farid Ghosn, and Mohamed Fawzi light monologues and sketches. After years of using foreign adaptations, Gaheli and Mohamed el-Bakar finally created original soundtracks.

The booming musicals energized the industry. Film production doubled from 30 films in 1944 to 60 films in 1946, creating the need for more studios.

Ahmed Galal and Mary Queeny split from Assia and established Studio Galal in 1944. Mohsen Szabo founded Studio Shubra. Studio Al-Ahram was established in 1945 by a group of Egyptians and foreigners, including Armenian Egyptian Hagop Ohan. Ohan planned the construction of Studio Al-Ahram and manufactured local movie cameras used by the studio for years. Nahas Film founded their own studio in 1948.

Seven studios operated during this decade, most offering full services. Foreigners ran the technical departments prior to their mass exodus after the 1956 Suez War.

A generation of filmmakers emerged that would influence the industry for the next five decades. Henri Barakat replaced Ahmed Galal as director of Assia's films in 1942. Salah Abu Seif, after editing at Studio Misr and directing some of its documentary films, made his first film in 1946. Hassan el-Imam, who started as an actor with the Ramses Troupe and then wrote sketches and assisted Niazi Mustafa and Ahmed Galal, made his first film in 1946. Helmi Rafla, a make-up artist in the 1930s and 1940s, assisted Togo Mizrahi on his last film and directed his first in 1947, as did Ezz-Eddine Zulficar after assisting Mohamed Abdel Gawad. Fateen Abdel Wahab made his first film in 1949 after assisting Yousef Wahbi and Ahmed Salem. Anwar Wagdi became actor, producer, and director and continued the *Laila* series with Laila Mourad after Togo Mizrahi left Egypt like many other Jews.

As a director, Yousef Wahbi made many successful films like *Passion and Revenge* (1944). In the early 1940s, he partnered with Mizrahi when the latter relocated to Cairo and used Studio Wahbi in Giza. They made four films starring Wahbi and Laila Mourad. Then he partnered with Nahas Films after Mizrahi's departure. Studio Nahas was built on land he owned in Giza.

According to doyen cinematographer Abdel Halim Nasr, the image was what was best in Egyptian cinema. His younger brother, Mahmoud Nasr, became a cinematographer in 1942 after assisting him in several films. Both were alumni of the Orfanelli school. Studio Misr trained a number of cinematographers, notably Ahmed Khorshed, Abdel Aziz Fahmi, Wahid Farid, and Hassan Dahesh.

The change in infrastructure was reflected in increased production, the largest in its history: from 96 films during the 1930s to 362 films in the 1940s. Cinema theaters, still controlled by foreigners, increased from 184 in 1947 to 244 two years later.

Transformation (1952–1963)

Days after the Free Officers came to power in July 1952, they summoned filmmakers and asked them to anoint the officers' coup on the silver screen. Officer Wagih Abaza asked them to abandon what he called "the cinema of buffoonery, song and dance." Producer-distributor Gabriel Talhami retorted it was a matter of supply and demand.

Until then, the government's role in the industry was limited to the Interior Ministry censoring or confiscating films deemed an affront to "Egypt's reputation," and enforcing the Entertainment Tax imposed in the mid-1930s. By the 1950s, the state "advised," occasionally threatened, and then transferred the Cinema Department from the Ministry of Social Affairs to the newly formed Ministry of National Guidance (now the Ministry of Culture) headed by writer Fathi Radwan.

The industry flirted with the new status quo. It changed its heroes from aristocrats—now villains—to the gallant commoner and the savior officer. But it could not produce the desired political propaganda, except in a few cases with state support such as *God Is with Us* (1955), *Revive My Heart* (1957), and *Port Said* (1957).

The government created the Cinema Support Organization under the Ministry of National Guidance in 1957, but it remained circumscribed in a vibrant film market.

In the early 1950s, a growing educated bourgeois class flocked to cinemas. In 1953, viewership at Cinema Metro, the principal venue for foreign films, reached 1.5 million, and half a million at Cinema

Cursal, the main playhouse for Egyptian films. Cairo's audience, the most educated, preferred foreign films, leading some filmmakers to urge the new nationalist government to support the local industry by imposing restrictions on foreign movies.

Filmmakers asked the government for official participation in international film festivals, offering to pay the expenses. In March 1952, the first official Egyptian delegation attended Cannes Festival with two films, *Son of the Nile* (1951) and *Night of Passion* (1951). The producers, Mary Queeny and Abdel Halim Nasr, bore the LE 1,500 cost of the trip.

The 1940s directors had turned a new corner.

Salah Abu Seif discovered Naguib Mahfouz as a screenwriter—a leap, he said, for the Egyptian screenplay. They collaborated on six of the 13 films directed by Abu Seif during the decade, including *A Woman's Youth* (1956), starring Taheya Carioca, which was well received at the 1956 Cannes Festival.

Kamal el-Sheikh, after years of editing, emerged as an innovative director with 16 films during the decade. His *Life or Death* (1954) screened at 1955 Cannes Festival.

Ezz-Eddine Zulficar, the most prolific of the decade, made 25 films. He was followed by Barakat, who evolved from the spectacle to romantic musicals starring Farid el-Atrash, before pairing with Faten Hamama to make social melodrama films.

Fateen Abdel Wahab emerged in the mid-1950s as a master of comedy films. With star Ismail Yassin, they achieved the highest earnings of the day. As a former army officer, Abdel Wahab was able to film in military locations, producing a series of light comedy films on the police, army, and navy that bore Ismail Yassin's name.

A new generation of young directors emerged. Yousef Chahine and Tewfik Saleh charted new cinematic territory. Action films by Hossam-Eddine Mustafa and Atef Salem attracted wide audiences, rivalling musicals and comedies at the box office.

The 1940s spectacle musical was replaced by romantic musicals again, enhanced by a young Abdel Halim Hafez whose first appearance was in a concert celebrating six months of the Free Officers' coup. He became a favorite of the time. Mohamed Abdel Wahab composed a song that Hafez sang on national radio to great acclaim. Abdel Wahab then announced Hafez's forthcoming film debut.

Stars of the previous era struggled to compete with the new blood. Mohamed Fawzi failed to stay on top of the box office. Laila Mourad faced accusations questioning her patriotism and faith. The films of Abdel Aziz Mahmoud and Karem Mahmoud produced by Hussein Fawzi and Abbas Kamel, once box office hits, were on the decline.

The Lama Brothers saga ended with Ibrahim Lama killing himself and his wife. Aziza Amir's career was cut short by her death. Hussein Sidki wore a military uniform to a filmmakers' meeting with the new officer-leaders, but the days of his films were over.

A few 1940s filmmakers persevered. Assia settled into her role as a professional producer, betting on new directors and ideas. Mary Queeny, after the sudden death of Ahmed Galal, managed their studio, producing for young Yousef Chahine, who had recently returned from the United States. Anwar Wagdi, after Laila Mourad's star had waned, moved to light comedies with the child star Fairouz. Helmi Rafla produced and directed seven films in 1954.

New producers emerged: Ramses Naguib in 1957 after training with 1940s directors; Gamal el-Leithy, originally from the Free Officers' propaganda department, laid the groundwork for nationalizing the industry; Hassan el-Saifi was one of the most prolific producer-directors in Egyptian cinema.

Despite the transformation, the 1950s ranked second in output with 530 films.

Sequestration (1963–1970)

The film industry suffered the fate of other industries: sequestration. The propaganda was clear. Egypt needed a socialist cinema that addressed the people's issues, stated Saad-Eddine Wahba, an architect of the film industry's sequestration.

Studio Misr went first in 1960 when Banque Misr and its companies were sequestered. The industry's infrastructure followed in 1963, inspired by the Soviet model.

It was an indiscriminate strike at a blooming industry. Tharwat Okasha, a prominent culture minister of the Nasser era, said that until his departure in 1962 there were no clear intentions to sequester cinema.

The major studios, film labs, and theaters the government sequestered were placed under the new General Organization of Cinema. Filmmakers like Salah Abu Seif, Naguib Mahfouz, Gamal el-Leithy, and Saad-Eddine Wahba were appointed to manage the organization. They were all witnesses in the Prosecutor General's investigation into its losses of over LE 6 million, nearly a decade later.

Yearly changes in the General Organization management system during the sequestration's nine years caused the collapse of the industry's infrastructure.

Studios and labs suffered neglect. Mary Queeny, who before sequestration had imported for Studio Galal Egypt's first color lab, saw it molder in a Studio Misr warehouse awaiting approval for release by an inflated bureaucracy where salaries consumed half the budget.

Cinema theaters deteriorated, particularly third-class theaters, decreasing from a high of 400 in the 1950s to 263. No new companies were established during the nine years for fear of sequestration.

But a special relationship blossomed between cinema and literature. Mohamed Hussein Haikal's novel *Zeinab* was adapted first as a silent film in 1930 and later as a talkie in the 1952, but cinema had generally stayed away from literature. In the mid-1960s, Egyptian filmmakers turned to novels, making 97 films during the sequestration period, mostly public sector productions.

Egypt was reaping the gains of the cultural and intellectual renaissance of the 1940s and 1950s. And a new generation of writers, unable to earn a decent living writing literature, turned to screenplays, as attested by Naguib Mahfouz.

Ehsan Abdel Koddous was the most prolific with 43 films adapted from his novels. He also wrote some of their screenplays. Next came Naguib Mahfouz with 41 films. Mahfouz started by writing screenplays then stories. He then wrote screenplays of other authors' novels, but categorically refused to write for his own.

The era's films went through phases. They began with patriotic political propaganda like *A Man in Our House* (1961), *Saladin* (1963), *Soft Hands* (1963), and *No Time for Love* (1963); followed by social drama about social injustice before the times of the Free Officers, like *The Forbidden* (1965) and *The Second Wife* (1967); progressive social drama like *Shame* (1967) and *My Wife, the General Manager* (1966); culminating, between the 1967 defeat and the 1971 demise of the public sector, with light comedies starring comedian Fuad el-Mohandes.

During the sequestration period, the private sector produced 281 films, its lowest output since the 1930s, because of the fear of sequestration, the exodus of producers to Lebanon in search of an alternative market, and the self-imposed exile of actors escaping security restrictions. The General Organization of Cinema produced 157 films.

Some film historians believe that milestones like Shadi Abdel Salam's *The Mummy* (1969) that garnered global attention, Tewfik Saleh's *Diary of a Rural Inspector* (1969), Yousef Chahine's *The Land* (1970), Barakat's *The Forbidden* (1965), Salah Abu Seif's *Cairo 30* (1966), would not have been made without the General Organization of Cinema. The historical and cinematic value of these films, they argued, transcended the financial loss that private companies might have sustained.

The 1967 military defeat offered an opening. Students protested against Nasser's rule. A wave of films like *A Touch of Fear* (1969) and *Miramar* (1969) delved into the causes of defeat. A new generation of directors proclaimed mutiny. The 1968 New Cinema Association declared that Egyptian cinema was presenting a "false reality."

Open Door (1973–1980)

With Anwar Sadat as president, sequestration was reversed. The General Organization of Cinema was dismantled in 1971. Standing on the ruins, the film industry was at a crossroad.

The state still appropriated all it had confiscated, but private enterprise had no fear of new sequestration, allowing it room to grow. The government created the Cinema, Theatre, and Music Authority in 1971, extending loans to private companies. At least 124 new film productions companies were formed based on these loans, but only five survived after the first film.

It was also a decade of endings.

Lotus Film, founded by pioneering Assia fifty years earlier, incurred unprecedented losses following the production of *Saladin*. She complained that the General Organization had asked to keep film copies to market and distribute but failed to execute the plan properly and didn't even give her the proceeds. She worked as an executive producer for the public sector, and when it was terminated, tried to resume her own production. But financial loss continued to hound her until she finally retired in 1972.

The Nile Film Company founded by Gabriel and Michel Talhami closed after 30 years of production and distribution. Helmi Rafla's company closed in the mid-1970s. He, too, had worked in the public sector, and his return to private enterprise was unsuccessful. In 1974, Ramses Naguib's company closed after 25 years in business.

The infrastructure had broken down. Studios and labs lacked regular maintenance. Theaters decayed and dwindled to no more than 200. Third-class cinemas disappeared. The Chamber of Film Industry decreed that a film was to remain in theaters as long as it earned minimum revenues, leading to films staying in storage for lack of theaters—or the "canister films" phenomena. *Look After Zoozoo* (1972) and *Bamba Kashar* (1974) screened for a whole year, while new films were shown years after their production, causing financial loss.

With the change of regime, there was a frenzy of movies critical of Nasser's rule. The government had launched what it called the Corrective Revolution in 1971. Cinema was in step, with what came to be known as *Karnaka* films, a reference to *Karnak* (1975) directed by Ali Badrakhan and based on a Naguib Mahfouz novel that was a scathing attack on Nasser's security services. Similar films followed: *Barefoot on a Golden Bridge* (1976), *Melancholy Night Bird* (1977), *Beyond the Sun* (1978), and *We're the Bus Passengers* (1979).

The anti-Nasserism wave did not mean there was no censorship. Yousef Chahine's *The Sparrow* (1972), which addressed popular anger over the 1967 military defeat to Israel, was banned and only permitted to screen two years later. *Visitor at Dawn* (1975) directed by Mamdouh Shoukry was banned for its daring treatment of state corruption. The director died after a long bout of depression after the censors insisted on chopping the film.

Hamam el-Malateely (1973) by Salah Abu Seif and *The Guilty Ones* (1975) by Said Marzouk battled with censorship and parliament over cuts to scenes deemed "morally indecent," foreshadowing Law 220 of 1976 that imposed new restrictions on cinema in the name of maintaining social stability and Egypt's reputation.

In the late 1960s, young Egyptian filmmakers coming of age were inspired by the 1950s auteur movies in France and Italy. It manifested in their first works: *My Wife and the Dog* (1971) by Said Marzouk and the films of the New Cinema Group that were harassed or banned—*Convergence* (1977), *Madness of Youth* (1975), and *Shadows on the Other Side* (1974).

The older generation also kept up with the change and the national mood, agitated over the war with Israel, the breakdown of the public sector, and the new economic Open Door policy.

Yousef Chahine raised his existential and political issues in his auteur films *The Choice* (1971), *The Sparrow* (1974), *Return of the Prodigal Son* (1976), concluding the decade with his autobiographical *Alexandria Why?* (1979).

Kamal el-Sheikh's partnership with the new scriptwriter Raafat el-Mihi energized the seasoned director in *Sunset and Sunrise* (1970), *The Fugitive* (1974), and *Whom Should We Aim the Bullet At?* (1975).

Salah Abu Seif presented two compelling works, *Hamam el-Malateely*, about savage Cairo in the seventies, and *The Saqqa Died* (1977), about man, existence, and death.

Hassan el-Imam and Hossam-Eddine Mustafa competed for most prolific director, both producing three or four films a year. With

Look After Zoozoo, el-Imam moved from melodrama to the lives of dancers, his favorite theme for the decade. Mustafa developed his action films with the rising stars of the 1970s in *Devils at Sea* (1972) and *Devils on Holiday* (1973).

Niazi Mustafa invested in new comedy talent as the films of Fuad el-Mohandes ebbed. He tapped Adel Imam for the leading role of *In Pursuit of a Scandal* (1973) that made Imam a box office star and a still-continuing phenomenon. He also gave Mohamed Sobhi his first lead role in the comedy *My Dear Uncle Zizo* (1977).

Henri Barakat reinvented his 1940s romantic films, sometimes with new titles, until the return of Faten Hamama, who had fled the Nasser regime. Together they presented a new genre of social melodrama concerned with women's issues, like *The Fine Thread* (1971) and *Mouths and Rabbits* (1977).

Ali Badrakhan was the most prominent new filmmaker. The crisis surrounding his film *Karnak* was his right of passage with both the audience and critics. Samir Seif and Nader Galal, the son of Mary Queeny and Ahmed Galal, made action films. Ashraf Fahmi became both producer and director.

The New Cinema Association disappeared with the exception of a number of films by Mohamed Rady. Ali Abdel Khalek stumbled after his *A Song on the Passage* (1972). Raafat el-Mihi settled for script writing, not making any films until the early 1980s.

Films of the late 1970s reflected the direction of future production. Adel Imam and seductive Nadia el-Gindi films topped the box office. Ahmed el-Sabaawy, assistant director since the 1940s, emerged to herald "the age of Sabaawy" of light, low-budget films.

Contractors (1981–1997)

From promulgation to criminality—nine decades abridge the journey of cinema in cafés.

Cinema projections started in cafés before theaters were built. But in 1984, Law No. 60 criminalized screening video films in cafés without a permit from the Censors.

Police cracked down on cafés to protect the industry from collapse. But the only alternative to the moribund third-class theaters was the new video screenings that had reached villages and poor neighborhoods.

Between 1980 and 1997, the number of cinema theaters continued to dwindle. In the 1980s, they reached 161 and first-class theaters like Cinema Studio Misr were closed. By the mid 1990s, 141 theaters remained, mostly in Greater Cairo and Alexandria. Some provinces lost all their theaters.

In the late 1970s, a new law stipulated that a new cinema must be built in place of a demolished one. But the government did not enforce it when it sold its cinema assets to developers and watched as residential blocks and shopping malls were built instead.

In 1980, the Supreme Council for Culture was formed. The Misr Studios and Theaters Company, which controlled the largest part of cinema assets, valued then at LE 19 million, was put under the Council's jurisdiction. In the early 1990s, with the creation of the Public Business Sector, a Cinema Holding Company was formed as a preliminary step toward privatizing and reselling the asset—now reduced to real estate with historical value of the eroded industry.

The studios, mired in debt, went to filming video and TV serials, degenerating until filmmakers abandoned them. Cameras and lighting and sound equipment became obsolete. *Makhzan* or storage emerged as the alternative: studio technicians formed equipment shops, imported or locally made, to rent out by the day.

Film labs deteriorated to the extent that international film festivals refused some Egyptian films due to technical defects in the copies.

Video ruled the day and it begot contractor cinema.

Video technology developed in the mid-1970s. In the early 1980s, with the Open Door economic policy, duty free zones were inundated with millions of video copies of Karate, Samurai, Hollywood B movies, and Bollywood musicals, intersecting with Gulf petro-dollars and Arab investment in cinema production.

The time was ripe for a change in taste and a revolution in the culture of viewership.

Contractor cinema was coined to the figure of the crooked contractor in the corruption and freewheeling environment associated with the Open Door era. It produced poor, low-budget films with second-rate stars directed by studio technicians-turned-directors. Filming lasted two weeks in rented apartments or villas. The producers were small-time traders financed by loans from local video distribution companies and Lebanese or Gulf distributors. The films were sold in video format immediately after their first screening.

The professional producer was replaced by the foreign distributor who controlled production. He decided the product predicated on what the Gulf audience wanted.

Between 1980 and 1997, the new, fast-paced production saw unprecedented figures in the industry's history: 900 films, mostly contractors'. The year 1986 marked the highest screening in Egypt: 97 films.

In parallel, 179 production companies were formed over 17 years, again most disappearing after their first film.

The figures did not reflect on the decrepit industry. The profits were siphoned off by the adventurers and new dealers into other more lucrative consumer ventures.

The period marked the end of what had survived of the old production companies. Hassan el-Saifi Films, Galal and Mary Queeny Films, Ittihad Films, Gamal el-Leithy Films, and Farid Shawki's El-Aahd El-Gadid Films all closed.

A few new companies appeared, some operating for one or two decades: Al-Ahram Film & Video Company, Gergis Fawzi Films, Mohamed Mokhtar Films, the International Television & Cinema Company (Hassan el-Kalla), Screen 2000 (Safwat Ghatas), and El-Sobky Video Film.

A new crop of filmmakers emerged in the early 1980s.

With a portable camera on the street, away from decaying studios and rented apartments, Said Sheemy filmed *Sunstroke* (1980), Mohamed Khan's first film.

Khan, returned from film studies in England, made twelve films in the 1980s and five in the 1990s with average earnings and critical acclaim, especially after he reinvented Adel Imam and Soad Hosni, the stars of the day.

Atef el-Tayeb, coming from the world of Yousef Chahine and Shadi Abdel Salam, was his generation's most prolific, controversial, and banned director with 20 films from the early 1980s until his untimely death in 1996. His films achieved both commercial and critical success after *The Bus Driver* (1982).

Khairi Bishara went through several stages despite his small output. He returned to contemporary literature in *The Collar and the Bracelet* (1986), and presented what was considered the prelude to youth films with the day's most famous singers in *Bitter Day, Sweet Day* (1988), *Kaboria* (1990), and *Ice Cream in Gleem* (1992).

Daoud Abdel Sayed made one film in the 1980s before taking off in the 1990s. His *KitKat* (1991), from a contemporary novel, was a commercial and critical success.

Sherif Arafa began with experimental films like *The Dwarves Are Coming* (1986) that met with critical approval but flopped at the box office. In the early 1990s, he made blockbusters that were the kiss of life to superstar Adel Imam, starting with *Playing with the Big Guys* (1991).

The films of this group described the societal crises of the post-Open Door economy, returnees from the 1973 war, and the new classes in Egyptian society. Egyptian films returned to international festivals.

The industry withered from stagnation: 17 years of the same box office stars, the seventies generation confounded by its severed experience, the eighties generation had consumed its vitality. In 1997, Egyptian cinema crossed one hundred years and a new consequential date.

Change happened by chance. It was a lightning strike from the audience, picked up by new filmmakers, and it changed the map.

The revenues of *Ismailia Round Trip* (1997), described as a "naive" film, reached LE 18 million and ran in cinemas for one whole year, unprecedented as the films of major stars never grossed more than LE 6 million.

Its makers proclaimed a "clean" cinema devoid of kissing. The public mood of the 1990s abounded with extremist religious propaganda coupled with the phenomenon of retiring female stars and campaigns to sanction the arts and on-screen kissing.

The new filmmakers' focus was light comedy and young group leads with new stars and contemporary themes. Cinema returned to its old seductive ways.

After the economic space was primed, a number of film companies appeared, funded by Egyptian and Gulf money.

With the age of satellite television, a battle over Egyptian cinema's assets for television airing ensued. Thousands of film reels stored in the warehouses of the Sound & Light Company and satellite television owners were all that remained of the dream factory.

The Lobby Cards

La Reine du Music Hall (1936)
Badia Massabni
directed by Mario Volpe, produced by Badia Massabni

L.E. 100.000 (1936)
Amina Mohamed
produced and directed by Togo Mizrahi

Les Deux Banquiers (El Ezz Bahdala) (1937)
Shalom and Ahmed el-Haddad
produced and directed by Togo Mizrahi

Le Tresor Perdu (1938)
Badr Lama and Nazli Kamel
directed by Ibrahim Lama, produced by Condor Film

On a Rainy Night (1939)
Yousef Wahbi and Laila Mourad
directed by Togo Mizrahi, produced by The Egyptian Films Company (Togo Mizrahi)

Laila the Schoolgirl (1941)
Yousef Wahbi and Laila Mourad
directed by Togo Mizrahi, produced by The Egyptian Films Company (Togo Mizrahi)

Laila the Country Girl (1941)
Yousef Wahbi and Bishara Wakim
directed by Togo Mizrahi, produced by The Egyptian Films Company (Togo Mizrahi)

Saladin (1941)
Badr Lama
directed by Ibrahim Lama, produced by Condor Film

A Dangerous Woman (1941)
Assia and Abbas Fares
directed by Ahmed Galal, produced by Lotus Film (Assia)

Le Vagabond (1942)
Zaki Rostom
directed by Barakat, produced by Lotus Film (Assia)

The Accused (1942)
Assia and Ashraf Abaza
directed by Barakat, produced by Lotus Film (Assia)

The Fifth Suitor (1942)
Assia and Soraya Fakhri
directed by Ahmed Galal, produced by Lotus Film (Assia)

The Straight Path (1943)
Yousef Wahbi
directed by Togo Mizrahi, produced by The Egyptian Films Company (Togo Mizrahi)

The Sheikh's Daughter (1943)
Yehia Chahine
directed by Ahmed Kamel Morsi, produced by Arab Films Company

What Madness (1944)

directed by Barakat, produced by Lotus Film (Assia)

38

Nour-Eddine and the Three Sailors (1944)
Ali el-Kassar, Ismail Yassin and Ali Abdel Aal
directed by Togo Mizrahi, produced by The Egyptian Films Company (Togo Mizrahi)

All Lies (1944)

directed by Togo Mizrahi, produced by The Egyptian Films Company (Togo Mizrahi)

The Blacksmith's Son (1944)
Yousef Wahbi
directed by Yousef Wahbi, produced by The Egyptian Films Company (Togo Mizrahi)

Laila, Daughter of the Poor (1945)
Soliman Naguib and Bishara Wakim
directed by Anwar Wagdi, produced by The Egyptian Company (Anwar Wagdi & Co.)

The Mother (1945)
Amina Rizk
directed by Omar Gemeiey, produced by Gemeiey Films

Love Story (1945)
Amira Amir and Ibrahim Hammouda
directed by Kamal Selim and Mohamed Abdel Gawad, produced by The Egyptian Films Company (Togo Mizrahi)

Angels in Hell (1946)
Amina Rizk, Faten Hamama, and Soad Mekawi
directed by Hassan el-Imam, produced by El-Wadi Films

The Misogynist (1946)
Sabah and Mohamed Fawzi
directed by Abdel Fattah Hassan, produced by Arab Films Company

The Five Pounds (1946)
Abdel Halim Morsi, Shafik Nour-Eddine, and Abdel Aziz el-Gahili
directed by Hassan Helmi, produced by Nile Films

The Absentee Returns (1947)
Siham Rifki and Mokhtar Osman
directed by Ahmed Galal, produced by Galal Films (Mary Queeny & Ahmed Galal)

The Mind on Holiday (1947)
Laila Fawzi and Abdel Salam el-Nabulsi
directed by Helmi Rafla, produced by Mohamed Fawzi Films

Kiss Me, Father (1947)
Nour el-Hoda and Mohamed Fawzi
directed by Badrakhan, produced by Technicians' Union

She Was an Angel (1947)
Marie Queeny
directed by Abbas Kamel, produced by Galal Films (Mary Queeny & Ahmed Galal)

A Muddled Life (1948)
El-Sayed Bedeir
directed by Ahmed Salem, produced by Rabha Films

52

The Divorce of Soad Hanem (1948)
Akila Rateb and Anwar Wagdi
directed by Anwar Wagdi, produced by United Films Co. (Anwar Wagdi & Co.)

She Lived in Darkness (1948)
Amina Rizk
directed by el-Sayed Ziyada, produced by Sons of Upper Egypt Films

The Mistress of the House (1949)
Emad Hamdi and Zeinab Sidki
directed by Ahmed Kamel Morsi, produced by Lotus Film (Assia)

Captive of the Eyes (1949)
Mohamed el-Kahlawi and Houriya Mohamed
directed by Ibrahim Helmi, produced by Kahlawi Films

Hoda (1949)
Nour el-Hoda
directed by Helmi Rafla, produced by Helmi Rafla Films

58

Eve of the Feast (1949)
Shadia and Elias Moaddab
directed by Helmi Rafla, produced by United Films Co. (Anwar Wagdi & Co.)

A Dancer's Romance (1950)
Mohamed Fawzi and Nour el-Hoda
directed by Helmi Rafla, produced by Mohamed Fawzi Films

Ethics for Sale (1950)
Mahmoud Zulficar, Faten Hamama, and Mimi Chakib
directed by Mahmoud Zulficar, produced by Aziza Amir Films

Sang dans le desert (1950)
Emad Hamdi
directed by Gianni Vernuccio, produced by El-Gabry Films

Miss Mama (1950)
Mohamed Fawzi, Ismail Yassin, and Hussein Ibrahim
directed by Helmi Rafla, produced by Mohamed Fawzi Films

End of a Story (1951)
Liz and Lynn
directed by Helmi Rafla, produced by Mohamed Fawzi Films

Leilet el-Henna (1951)
Marie Mounib
directed by Anwar Wagdi, produced by United Films Co. (Anwar Wagdi & Co.)

Fairouz Hanem (1951)
Taheya Carioca, Fairouz, and Abdel Hamid Zaki
directed by Abbas Kamel, produced by United Films Co. (Anwar Wagdi & Co.)

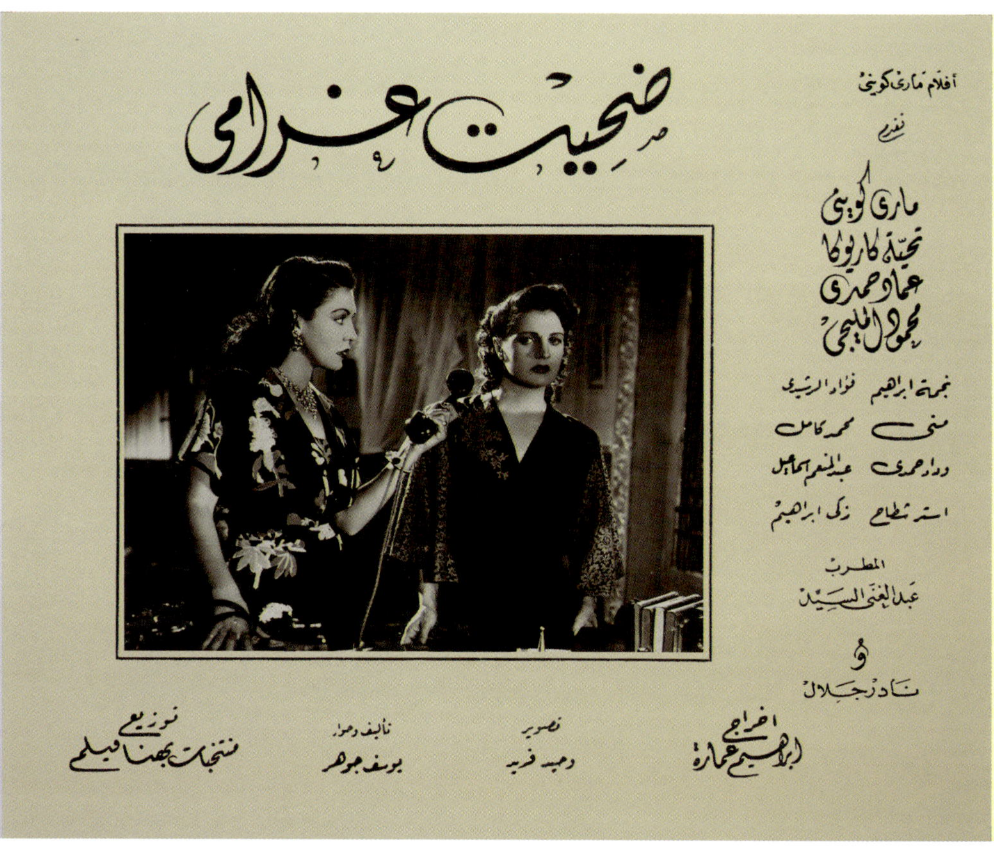

Victim of My Love (1951)
Marie Queeny and Taheya Carioca
directed by Ibrahim Omara, produced by Mary Queeny Films

Son of the Nile (1951)
Faten Hamama and Yehia Chahine
directed by Yousef Chahine, produced by Mary Queeny Films

L'Eternel Amour (1951)
Yousef Wahbi and Laila Mourad
directed by Anwar Wagdi, produced by United Films Co. (Anwar Wagdi & Co.)

Patience Is a Virtue (1951)
Mohamed el-Kahlawi and Houriya Hassan
directed by Niazi Mustafa, produced by Nahas Film

The Flowers of Love (1951)
Laila Mourad and Mohamed Fawzi
directed by Barakat, produced by Mohamed Fawzi Films

Don't Tell (1952)
Farid el-Atrash and Abdel Salam el-Nabulsi
directed by Barakat, produced by Farid el-Atrash Films

The Wrath of Parents (1952)

directed by Hassan el-Imam, produced by Arab Films Company

A Father's Mistake (1952)
Shadia, Mahmoud el-Meligi, and Aziz Osman
directed by Barakat, produced by Arab Films Company

I Believe in God (1952)
Aziza Amir, Mahmoud el-Meligi, Soheir, and Adel
directed by Mahmoud Zulficar, produced by Mahmoud Zulficar Films

Mustafa Kamel (1952)
Hussein Riyad
directed by Ahmed Badrakhan, produced by El-Masri Films

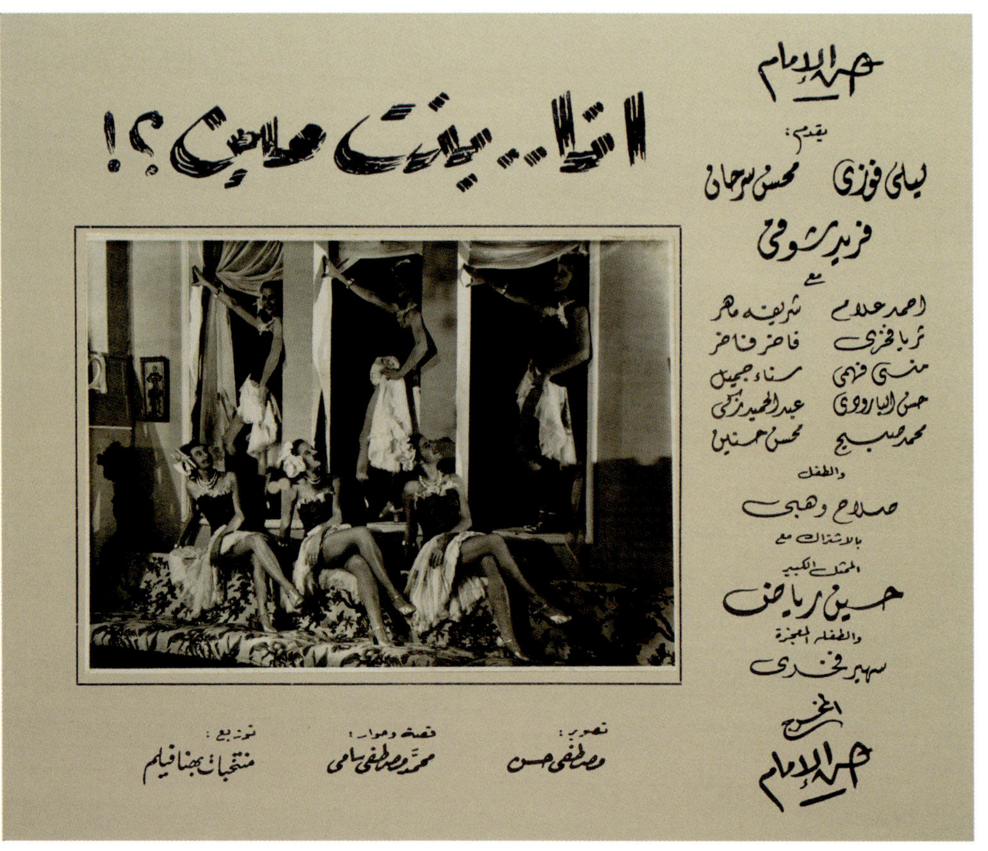

Whose Daughter Am I? (1952)

produced and directed by Hassan el-Imam

Melody to Eternity (1952)
Farid el-Atrash, Madiha Yousri, Faten Hamama, and Magda
directed by Barakat, produced by Misr Acting & Film Company

Fille de Notables (1953)
Laila Mourad and Ismail Yassin
directed by Anwar Wagdi, produced by United Films Co. (Anwar Wagdi & Co.)

The Board of Directors (1953)
Stefan Rosti and Hoda Shams-Eddine
directed by Abbas Kamel, produced by Anton Khoury Films

80

In Whose Law? (1953)
Magda and Hussein Riyad
directed by Hassan el-Imam, produced by Arab Films Company (Kamel Abdullah Hammouda and Co.)

Love in the Dark (1953)
Amina Rizk
produced and directed by Hassan el-Imam

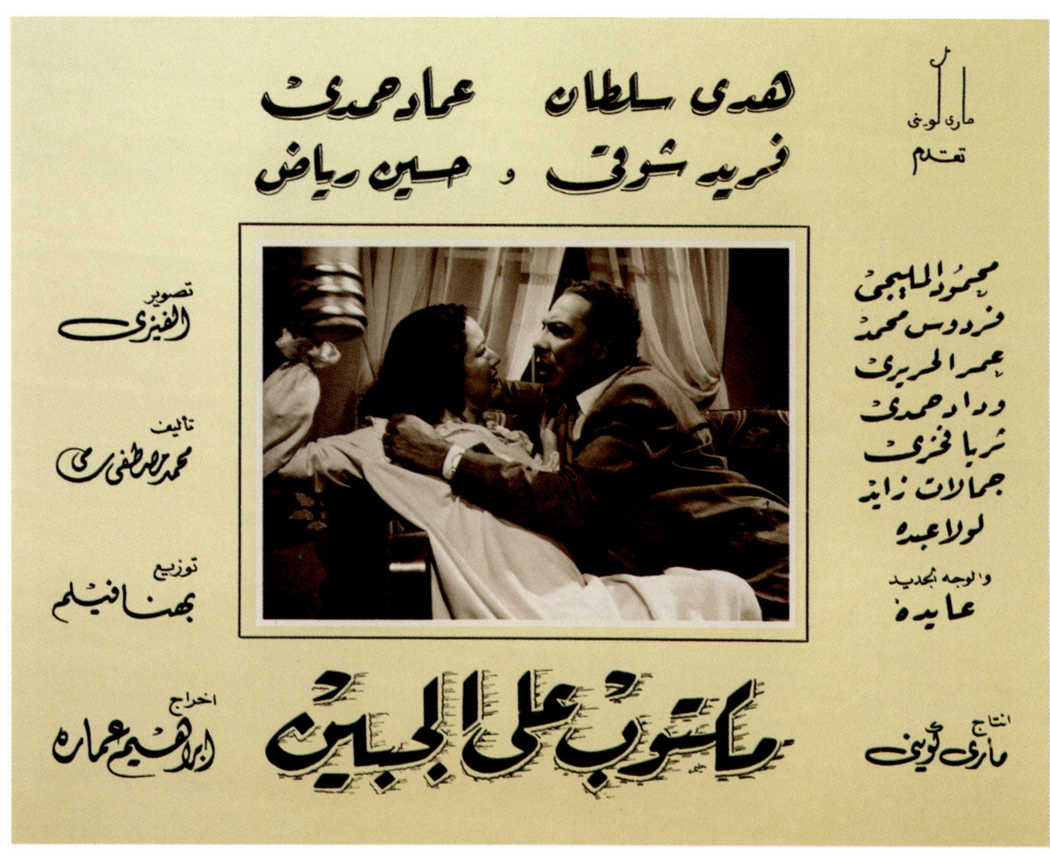

Written on the Forehead (1953)
Farid Shawki and Hoda Sultan
directed by Ibrahim Emara, produced by Mary Queeny

82

Your Tongue Is Your Horse (1953)
Shadia
directed by Abbas Kamel, produced by Mary Queeny

The Bread-Seller (1953)
Amina Rizk and Shadia
directed by Hassan el-Imam, produced by Gabriel Talhami and Mustafa Hassan

The Efrit of Uncle Abdou (1953)
Ismail Yassin, Habayeb, and Shukri Sarhan
directed by Hussein Fawzi, produced by Hussein Fawzi Films

Folie d'Amour (1954)
Rakia Ibrahim
produced and directed by Mohamed Karim

The Blazing Sun (1954)
Hamdi Gheith
directed by Yousef Chahine, produced by Gabriel Talhami

You Only Have One Life (1954)
Ismail Yassin
directed by Ehsan Farghal, produced by Arab Films Company (Kamel Abdullah Hammouda and Co.)

Ma Bien Aimée (1954)
Naima Akef
directed by Hussein Fawzi, produced by Omayad Films (Zuheir Bakir and Co.)

Dark Angel (1954)

produced and directed by Hassan el-Imam

Always with You (1954)
Faten Hamama and Mohamed Fawzi
directed by Barakat, produced by Mohamed Fawzi Films

Women Don't Know How to Lie (1954)
Ismail Yassin and Zenat Sidki
directed by Abdel Gawad, produced by Azim Film

Country Girl (1954)
Kitty and Mohamed el-Tabei (Abdel Rehim Kabir el-Rehimiya Qibli)
directed by Hassan el-Saifi, produced by Peace Films

93

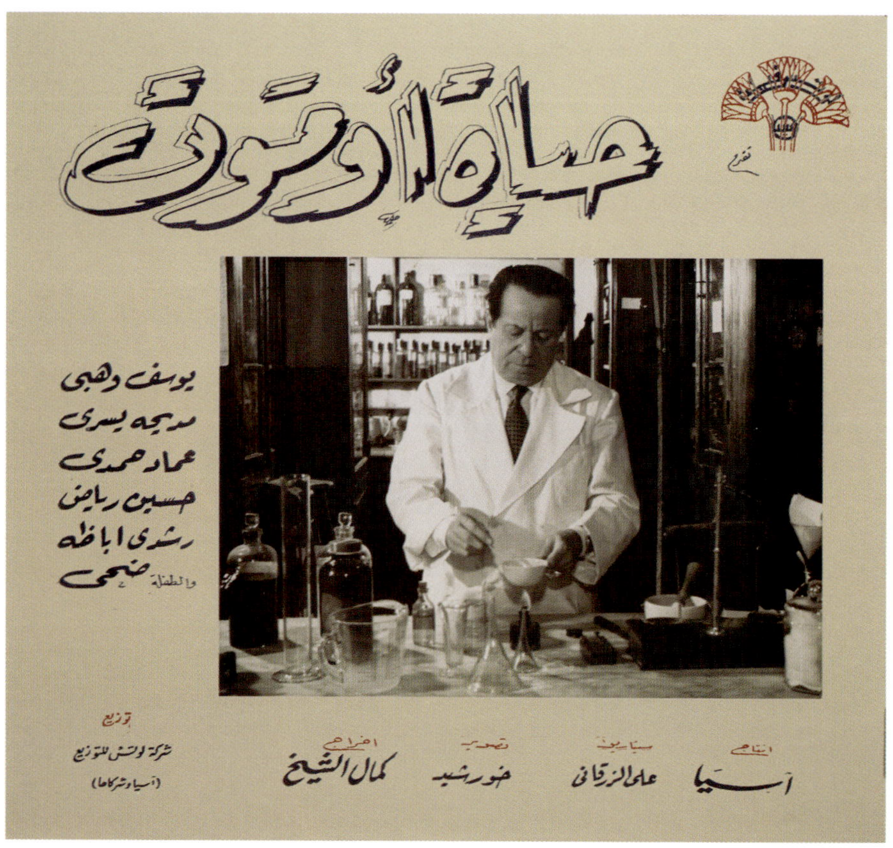

Life or Death (1954)
Hussein Riyad
directed by Kamal el-Sheikh, produced by Lotus Film (Assia)

Lovers' Village (1954)
Magda
directed by Ahmed Diaa-Eddine, produced by Yehia Chahine Films

Candy Doll (1954)

directed by Abbas Kamel, produced by Kassem Wagdi Films

Love Letter (1954)
Farid el-Atrash
directed by Barakat, produced by Farid el-Atrash Films

The Triumph of Love (1954)
Kamal el-Shinnawi
directed by Hassan Ramzi, produced by El-Nasr Films (Hassan Ramzi)

The Covenant of Love (1955)
Farid el-Atrash and Yousef Wahbi
directed by Ahmed Badrakhan, produced by Farid el-Atrash Films

The Missing Lady (1955)
Mariam Fakhr-Eddine and Mahmoud el-Meligi
directed by Ezz-Eddine Zulficar, produced by Mohamed Fawzi Films

Kingdom of Womcn (1955)

directed by Ehsan Farghal, produced by Kassem Wagdi Films

Melody of Fidelity (1955)
Abdel Halim Hafez
directed by Ibrahim Omara, produced by Ihab el-Leithy Films

God Is with Us (1955)
Magda
directed by Ahmed Badrakhan, produced by Arab Films

The Body (1955)
Mokhtar Osman
produced and directed by Hassan el-Imam

Call Girls (1955)
Madiha Yousri, Hamdi Gheith and Soraya Fakhri
directed by Hassan el-Imam, produced by Salam el-Intisar Film

Spring Dreams (1955)
Madiha Yousri, Kamal el-Shinnawi, and Zahret el-Ola
directed by Hassan Ramzi, produced by El-Nasr Films

Memory Beach (1955)
Shadia and Shukri Sarhan
directed by Ezz-Eddine Zulficar, produced by Shadia and Emad Hamdi Films

The Revolt of the City (1955)
Mohamed Fawzi
directed by Helmi Rafla, produced by Lotus Film (Assia)

Devils of the Air (1956)
Abdel Salam el-Nabulsi and Said Abu Bakr
directed by Niazi Mustafa, produced by El-Nagah Films

Who's the Murderer? (1956)
Hussein Riyad and Amina Nour-Eddine
directed by Hassan el-Saifi, produced by Lotus Film (Assia)

Love and Humanity (1956)
Abdel Salam el-Nabulsi
directed by Hussein Fawzi, produced by Hussein Fawzi Films

111

Nimrod (1956)
Farid Shawki
directed by Atef Salem, produced by El-Aahd El-Gadid Films

Confused Hearts (1956)
Zahret el-Ola and Mahmoud el-Meligi
directed by Ibrahim Omara, produced by Arab Films Company (Kamel Abdullah Hammouda and Co.)

La Nuit Sans Fin (1956)
Shadia and Salah Zulficar
directed by Ezz-Eddine Zulficar, produced by Gabriel Talhami

The Heart Has Rules (1956)
Zenat Sidki and Abdel Fattah el-Kosari
directed by Helmi Halim, produced by The Arabic Film

How Can I Forget You (1956)
Farid el-Atrash and Sabah
directed by Badrakhan, produced by Farid el-Atrash Films

Farewell to Your Love (1956)
Farid el-Atrash and Shadia
directed by Yousef Chahine, produced by Farid el-Atrash Films

Women in My Life (1957)
Hind Rostom
directed by Fateen Abdel Wahab, produced by Yehia Chahine Films

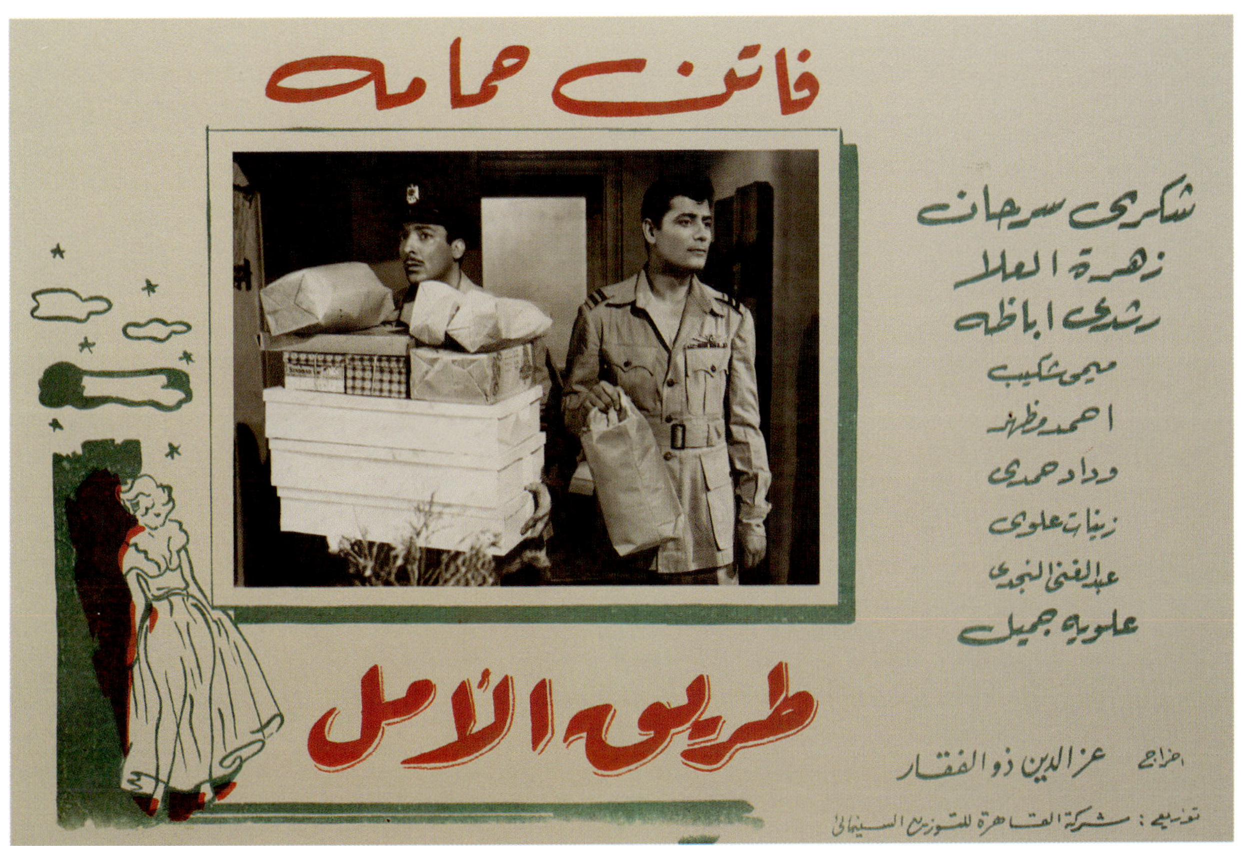

The Road of Hope (1957)
Shukri Sarhan and Rushdi Abaza
directed by Ezz-Eddine Zulficar, produced by Helmi Rafla Films

The Land of Peace (1957)
Omar Sharif
directed by Kamal el-Sheikh, produced by The Arabic Film

120

Tamarind (1957)
Naima Akef and Rushdi Abaza
directed by Hussein Fawzi, produced by Hussein Fawzi Films

Salutations to the Loved Ones (1958)
Sabah
directed by Helmi Halim, produced by The Arabic Film

Ghariba (1958)
Nagat el-Sagheera and Ahmed Ramzi
directed by Ahmed Badrakhan

The Dead End (1958)
Faten Hamama
directed by Salah Abu Seif, produced The Arab Cinema Company

My Happy Days (1958)
Hassan Fayek and Gawaher
directed by Ahmed Diaa-Eddine, produced by Diaa-Eddine

This is Love (1958)
Yehia Chahine and Abdel Moneim Ibrahim
directed by Salah Abu Seif, produced by Ramses Naguib

The Lady of the Palace (1958)
Faten Hamama and Omar Sharif
directed by Kamal el-Sheikh, produced by Filmmakers' Union Film Company (Hassan Ramzi and Co.)

Thinking of the One Who Jilted Me (1959)
Rushdi Abaza
produced and directed by Hossam-Eddine Mustafa

Have Mercy on My Love (1959)
Shadia and Mariam Fakhr-Eddine
directed by Barakat, produced by Helmi Rafla

The Green Threshold (1959)
Sabah
directed by Fateen Abdel Wahab, produced by Andalus Film

Surprise Hotel (1959)
Hind Rostom
directed by Issa Karama, produced by El-Aalam El-Gadid Films (Mustafa Hassan and Co.)

Story of a Love Affair (1959)
Abdel Halim Hafez
produced and directed by Helmi Halim

Dreams of Girls (1959)
Berlanti Abdel Hamid, Shukri Sarhan, and Abdel Salam el-Nabulsi
directed by Yousef Maalouf, produced by Nahas Films

The Poor Millionaire (1959)
Ismail Yassin and Faiza Ahmed
directed by Hassan el-Saifi, produced by Mary Queeny

Ismail Yassin in the Air Force (1959)
Ismail Yassin and Riyad el-Qasabgi
directed by Fateen Abdel Wahab, produced by The Arab Cinema Company

136

The Secret of the Invisibility Cap (1959)

directed by Niazi Mustafa, produced by The Arab Cinema Company

My Wife's Bridegroom (1959)
Ismail Yassin and Loula Sidki
directed by Abbas Kamel, produced by Loula Sidki Films

The Love Nest (1959)
Kamal el-Shinnawi
directed by Helmi Rafla, produced by Kamal el-Shinnawi Films

The Sun Never Sets (1959)
Zubaida Sarwat
directed by Hussein Helmi, produced by El-Nasr Films (Hassan Ramzi)

The Police Inspector (1959)
Yousef Wahbi and Rushdi Abaza
directed by Hussein Fawzi, produced by Hussein Fawzi Films

My Mother-in-Law Is an Angel (1959)
Marie Mounib and Yousef Fakhr-Eddine
directed by Issa Karama, produced by Karama Film

The Second Man (1959)
Samia Gamal
directed by Ezz-Eddine Zulficar, produced by Ezz-Eddine Zulficar Films

Struggle on the Nile (1959)
Hind Rostom
directed by Atef Salem, produced by Gamal el-Leithy Films

I Accuse (1960)
Zizi el-Badrawi and Emad Hamdi
directed by Hassan el-Imam, produced by Al-Mansoura Films (Wali & Co.)

Kaiss and Laila (1960)
Magda and Shukri Sarhan
directed by Ahmed Diaa-Eddine, produced by Gabriel Talhami

Love and Worship (1960)
Taheya Carioca and Salah Zulficar
directed by Hassan el-Imam, produced by Dinar Film

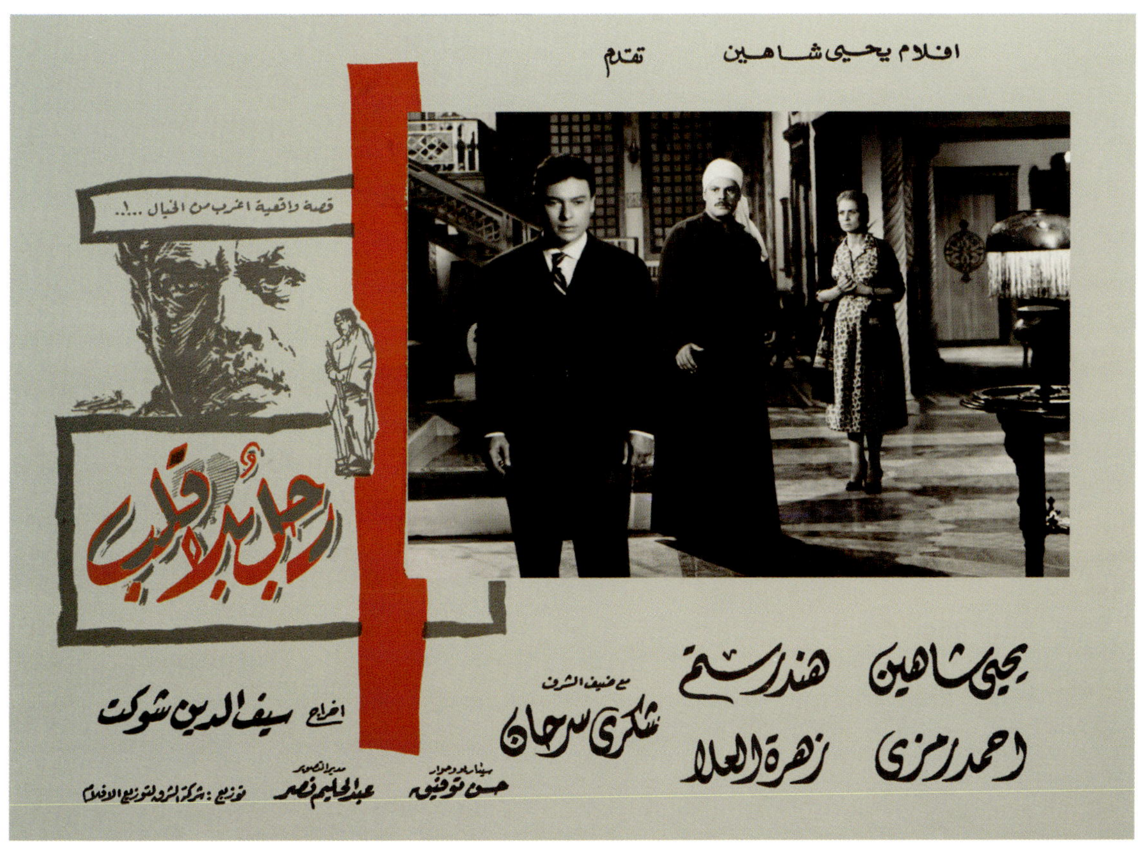

A Man without a Heart (1960)
Yehia Chahine, Ahmed Ramzi and Zahret el-Ola
directed by Seif-Eddine Chawkat, produced by Yehia Chahine Films

The Melody of Happiness (1960)
Muharram Fuad, Iman, Abdel Moneim Ibrahim, Hussein Riyad, and Magda el-Khatib
directed by Helmi Rafla, produced by Helmi Rafla Films

My Beloved's Anklet (1960)
Naima Akef and Rushdi Abaza
directed by Hassan Reda, produced by Helmi Rafla Films

My Only Love (1960)
Omar Sharif
directed by Kamal el-Sheikh, produced by Gamal el-Leithy Films

A Woman's Secret (1960)
Hoda Sultan
directed by Atef Salem, produced by Al-Shams Films (A. Gabbour)

The River of Love (1960)
Omar Sharif and Fuad el-Mohandes
directed by Ezz-Eddine Zulficar, produced by Helmi Rafla Films

The Seven Girls (1961)
Nadia Lotfi, Zizi el-Badrawi, and Soad Hosni
directed by Atef Salem, produced by Helmi Rafla Films

Don't Remember Me (1961)
Shadia and Stefan Rosti
directed by Mahmoud Zulficar, produced by The Arab Cinema Company

A Day of My Life (1961)
Abdel Halim Hafez and Zubaida Sarwat
directed by Atef Salem, produced by El-Mutahida Cinema

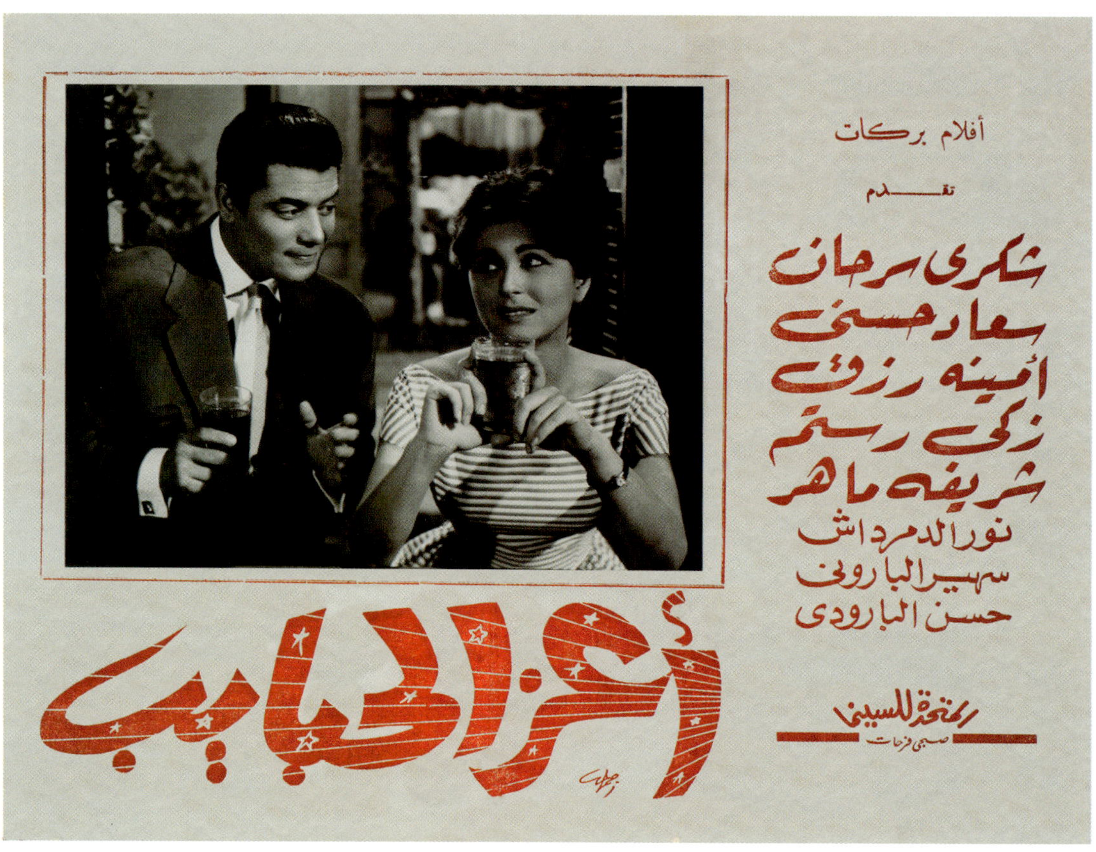

Most Beloved (1961)
Soad Hosni and Shukri Sarhan
directed by Barakat, produced by Barakat Films

Ashour the Lionhearted (1961)
Taheya Carioca
directed by Hussein Fawzi, produced by Rushdi Abaza

The Road of Tears (1961)
Kamal el-Shinnawi
directed by Helmi Halim, produced by Kamal el-Shinnawi Films

The Day of Judgment (1962)
Samira Ahmed
directed by Abdel Rahman Sherif, produced by Kamal Salah-Eddine Films

Salwa in the Wind (1962)
Zubaida Sarwat and Shukri Sarhan
directed by El-Sayed Bedeir, produced by Ibrahim Wali

Beware of Eve (1962)
Lobna Abdel Aziz, Rushdi Abaza, and Hussein Riyad
directed by Fateen Abdel Wahab, produced by Ramses Naguib

The Miracle (1962)
Hussein Riyad
directed by Hassan el-Imam, produced by Helmi Rafla Films

Saladin (1963)
Ahmed Mazhar
directed by Yousef Chahine, produced by Lotus Film (Assia) with the General Organization of Cinema

Zizi's Family (1963)
Ahmed Ramzi, Laila Shoeir, and Adli Kasseb
directed by Fateen Abdel Wahab, produced by Al-Ittihad Films (Abbas Helmi)

Cairo by Night (1963)

directed by Mohamed Salem, produced by The General Company for Arab Cinema Production

The Bridegroom Arrives Tomorrow (1963)
Soad Hosni
directed by Niazi Mustafa, produced by Mounir Rafla

The Last Night (1963)
Faten Hamama and Ahmed Mazhar
directed by Kamal el-Sheikh, produced by Gamal el-Leithy Films

Amongst the People (1964)
Samira Ahmed and Hassan Yousef
directed by Kamal Attiya, produced by Star Film (Tewfik el-Sabahi)

The Game of Love and Marriage (1964)
Soad Hosni, Soheir el-Babli, and Farid Shawki
directed by Niazi Mustafa, produced by Mounir Rafla

169

A Distinguished Family (1964)
Hoda Sultan and Adel Adham
directed by Fateen Abdel Wahab, produced by The General Company for Arab Cinema Production (Filmintag)

If I Were a Man (1964)
Aida Hilal
directed by Ahmed Diaa-Eddine, produced by Aida Hilal Films

A Thousand and One Nights (1964)
Shadia and Yousef Shaaban
directed by Hassan el-Imam, produced by Mounir Rafla Films

A Husband on Vacation (1964)
Salah Zulficar and Laila Taher
directed by Mohamed Abdel Gawad, produced by The General Company for Arab Cinema Production

Talk of the Town (1964)
Chewikar
directed by Kamal Attiya, produced by Magda Films

174

For Hanafi (1964)
Ahmed Ramzi
directed by Hassan el-Saifi, produced by The General Company for Arab Cinema Production

Love, Fun, and Youth (1964)
Nadia Lotfi and Yousef Fakhr-Eddine
directed by Nagdi Hafez, produced by Borg al-Qahira Films

Confessions of a Husband (1964)
Fuad el-Mohandes, Chewikar, and Marie Mounib
directed by Fateen Abdel Wahab, produced by The General Company for Arab Cinema Production

177

For Men Only (1964)
Soad Hosni and Nadia Lotfi
directed by Mahmoud Zulficar, produced by Gamal el-Leithy Films

178

The Unknown Man (1965)
Zizi el-Badrawi, Salwa Mahmoud, and Salah Kabil
directed by Mohamed Abdel Gawad, produced by The General Company for Arab Cinema Production

Alamein (1965)
Salah Kabil and Madiha Salem
directed by Abdel Alim Khattab, produced by The General Company for Arab Cinema Production

The Technical Director (1965)
Farid Shawki
directed by Fateen Abdel Wahab, produced by Ihab el-Leithy Films

Mind and Money (1965)
Ismail Yassin
directed by Abbas Kamel, produced by The General Company for Arab Cinema Production (Filmintag)

Dawn of a New Day (1965)
Sanaa Gamil and Yousef Chahine
directed by Yousef Chahine, produced by Galal Films

Completely Mad (1965)
Mohamed Awad
directed by Issa Karama, produced by Karama Film

Private Tutor (1965)
Emad Hamdi and Soheir Zaki
directed by Ahmed Diaa-Eddine, produced by Gomhouriya Film

Boys and Girls (1965)
Madiha Salem, Nawal Aboul Fotouh, Hassan Yousef, Nahed Sherif, and Nabil el-Zagzugi
directed by Hussein Helmi (El-Mohandes), produced by Dinar Film

The Mamelukes (1965)
Omar Sharif and Nabila Ebeid
directed by Atef Salem, produced by Cairo Cinema Company

All Three Love Her (1965)
Soad Hosni, Hassan Yousef, Nahed Sherif, and Yousef Fakhr-Eddine
directed by Mahmoud Zulficar, produced by Cairo Cinema Company

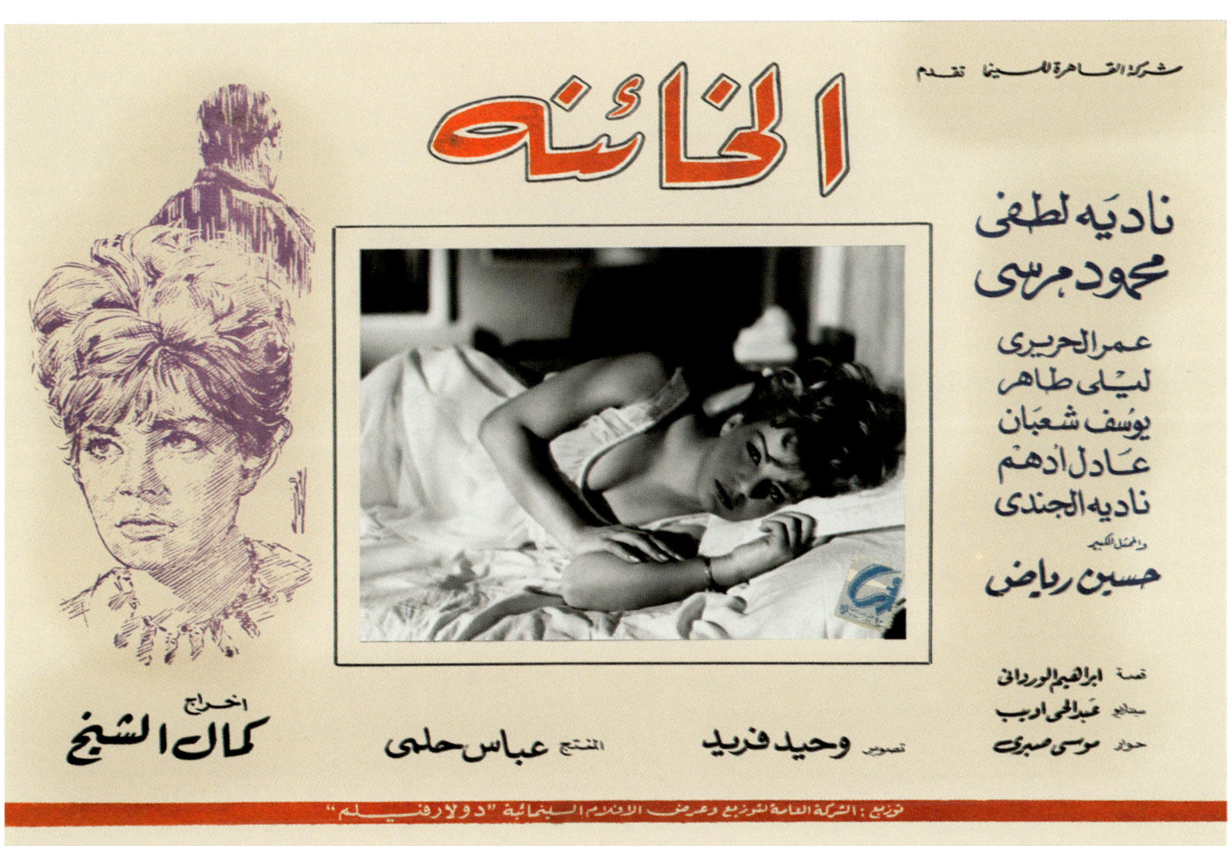

Unfaithful (1965)
Nadia Lotfi
directed by Kamal el-Sheikh, produced by Cairo Cinema Company

The Confession (1965)
Madiha Yousri
directed by Saad Arafa, produced by The General Company for Arab Cinema Production (Filmintag)

Khan el-Khalili (1966)
Samira Ahmed
directed by Atef Salem, produced by Cairo Cinema Company

My Wife, the General Manager (1966)
Shadia and Adel Imam
directed by Fateen Abdel Wahab, produced by The General Company for Arab Cinema Production (Filmintag)

Take Me with You (1966)
Samira Ahmed
directed by Abbas Kamel, produced by El-Mutahida Cinema (Sobhi Farahat)

Naughty Men (1966)
Samia Gamal and Rushdi Abaza
directed by Hossam-Eddine Mustafa, produced by Rushdi Abaza Films

The Wedding Night (1966)
Ahmed Mazhar and Soad Hosni
directed by Barakat, produced by Cairo Cinema Company

Something in My Life (1966)
Faten Hamama
directed by Barakat, produced by Cairo Cinema Company

The Revolution in Yemen (1966)
Salah Mansour, Emad Hamdi, and Abdel Azim Abdel Haq
directed by Atef Salem, produced by The General Company for Arab Cinema Production (Filmintag)

198

Sayed Darwish (1966)
Hind Rostom
directed by Ahmed Badrakhan, produced by The General Company for Arab Cinema Production (Filmintag)

A Wife from Baris (1966)
Rushdi Abaza and Nabila Ebeid
directed by Atef Salem, produced by Cairo Cinema Company

199

Cairo 30 (1966)
Soad Hosni, Tewfik el-Diqqin, and Hamdi Ahmed
directed by Salah Abu Seif, produced by Cairo Cinema Company

August Romance (1966)
Fuad el-Mohandes and Chewikar
directed by Hassan el-Saifi, produced by Abdel Kader el-Shinnawi Films

202

A Man and Two Women (1966)
Yehia Chahine and Samiha Ayoub
directed by Nagdi Hafez, produced by Peter Film

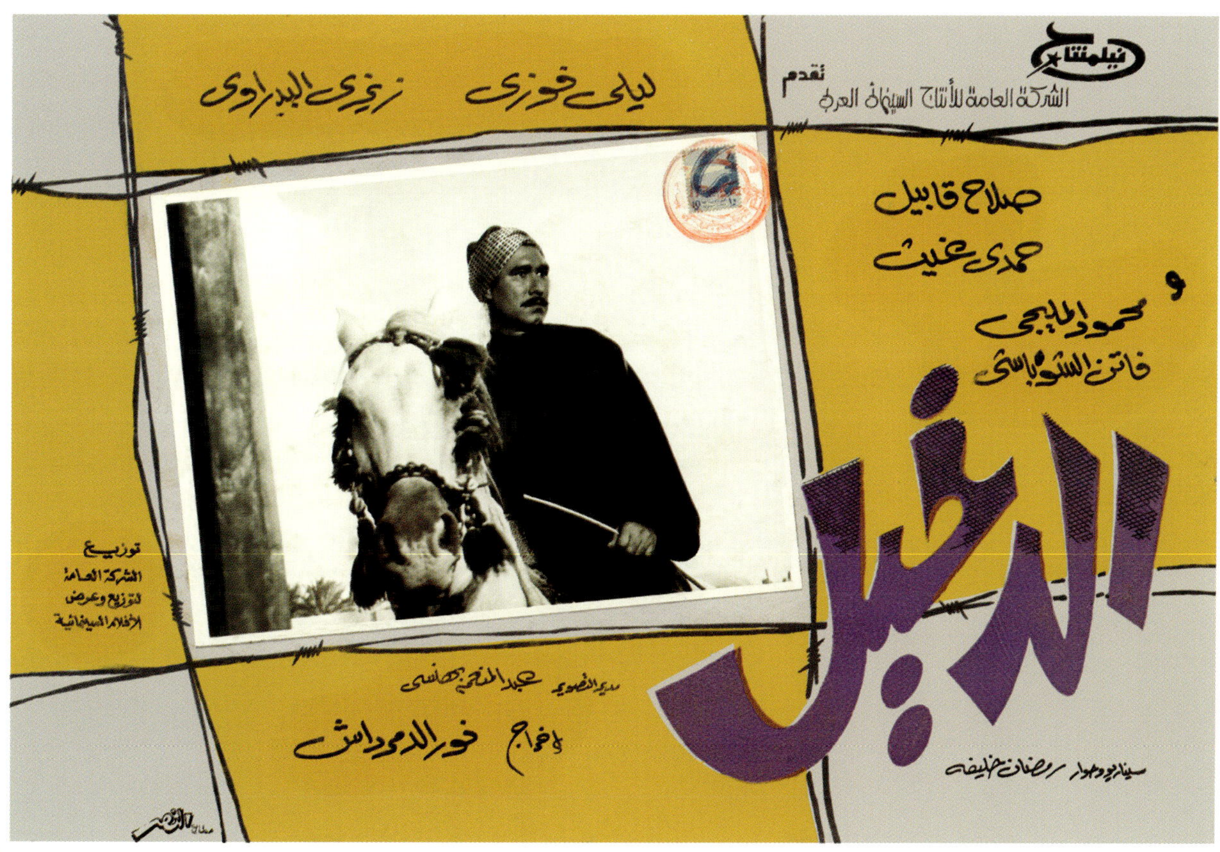

The Outsider (1967)
Hamdi Gheith
directed by Nour el-Demerdash, produced by The General Company for Arab Cinema Production (Filmintag)

The Drought (1967)
Ahmed el-Gezeiri and Morsi Khattab
directed by Sayed Issa, produced by Cairo Cinema Company

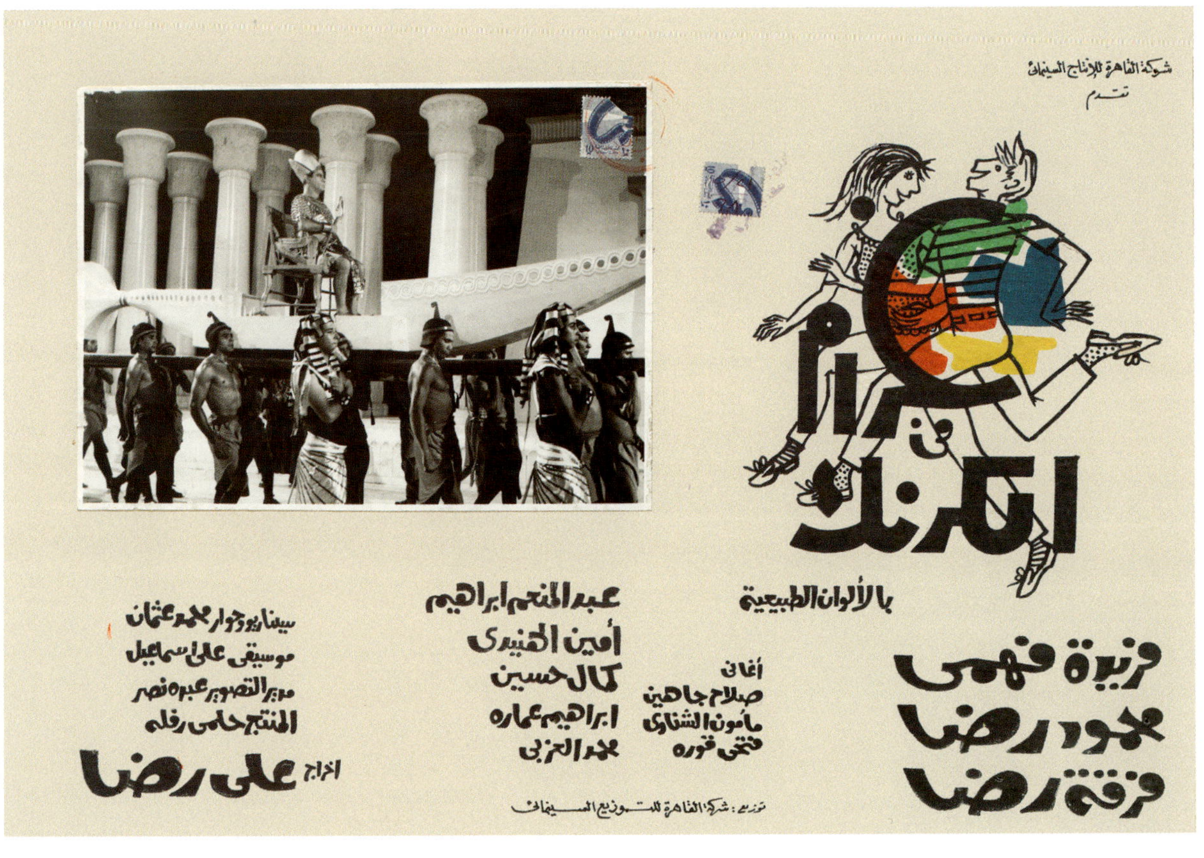

Romance in Karnak (1967)
Amin el-Henedi and the Reda Troupe
directed by Ali Reda, produced by Cairo Cinema Company

Shame (1967)
Lobna Abdel Aziz and Rushdi Abaza
directed by Galal el-Sharkawi, produced by Cairo Cinema Company

The Days of Love (1968)
Soheir el-Babli
directed by Helmi Halim, produced by Cairo Cinema Company

The Rebels (1968)
Shukri Sarhan, Tewfik el-Diqqin, Zizi Mustafa, and Mohamed Tewfik
directed by Tewfik Saleh, produced by The General Company for Arab Cinema Production (Filmintag)

The Land of Hypocrisy (1968)
Fuad el-Mohandes and Abdel Rehim el-Zorkani
directed by Fateen Abdel Wahab, produced by The General Organization of Cinema

The Lamp of Umm Hashem (1968)

directed by Kamal Attiya, produced by Cairo Cinema Company

One of the Girls (1968)
Magda el-Khatib
directed by Kamal Attiya, produced by Cairo Cinema Company

The Circus (1968)

directed by Atef Salem, produced by The General Organization of Cinema

The Diaries of a Provincial Prosecutor (1969)

directed by Tewfik Saleh, produced by The General Organization of Cinema

A Bit of Fear (1969)
Boussy and Amal Zayed
directed by Hussein Kamal, produced by The General Organization of Cinema

El-Sayed El-Bolti (1969)
Ezzat el-Alayli and Soheir el-Morshidi
directed by Tewfik Saleh, produced by The General Organization of Cinema

Miramar (1969)
Shadia and Yousef Shaaban
directed by Kamal el-Sheikh, produced by The General Organization of Cinema

The Mummy, or The Night of Counting the Years (1969)
Left: Nadia Lotfi and Ahmed Marei. Right: Ahmed Hegazy and Zouzou Hamdi el-Hakim
directed by Shadi Abdel Salam, produced by The General Organization of Cinema

Things That Can't Be Bought (1970)
Yehia Chahine and Shams el-Baroudi
directed by Ahmed Diaa-Eddine, produced by The General Organization of Cinema

Bridegroom of the Minister's Daughter (1970)
Fuad el-Mohandes, Salama Elias, Hussein Zayed, and Chewikar
directed by Niazi Mustafa, produced by Gamal el-Leithy Films

Escape (1970)
Farid Shawki and Yousef Shaaban
directed by Hassan Reda, produced by Ahmed Kamel Hefnawi

Sunset and Sunrise (1970)
Soad Hosni and Ibrahim Khan
directed by Kamal el-Sheikh, produced by The General Organization of Cinema

Reda Bond (1970)
Chewikar and Mahmoud el-Meligi
directed by Nagdi Hafez, produced by City Film (Farouk Naguib and Co.)

222

The Thief of the Piece of Paper (1970)
Mahmoud Reda and Farida Fahmi
directed by Ali Reda, produced by The General Organization of Cinema

Duel in Alamein (1970)
Nahed Sherif
directed by Hossam-Eddine Mustafa, produced by Ihab el-Leithy Films

Furnished Flat (1970)
Mohamed Reda
directed by Hassan el-Imam, produced by Hassan el-Imam Films

The Murderer of Women (1970)
Fuad el-Mohandes and Farouk Falawkas
directed by Niazi Mustafa, produced by Gamal el-Leithy Films

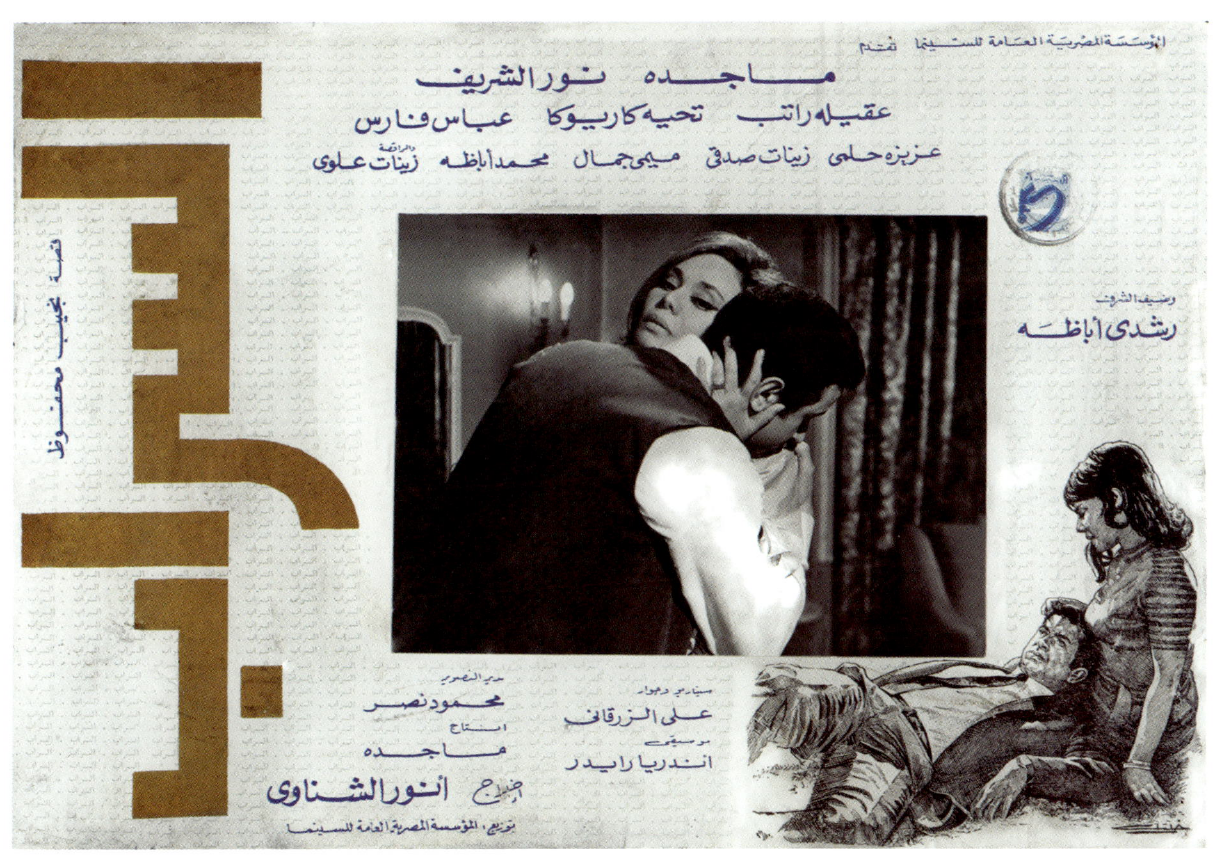

Mirage (1970)
Magda and Nour el-Sherif
directed by Anwar el-Shinnawi, produced by The General Organization of Cinema

Dawn of Islam (1971)
Nagwa Ibrahim and Samiha Ayoub
directed by Salah Abu Seif, produced by The General Organization of Cinema

The Choice (1971)
Soad Hosni
directed by Yousef Chahine, produced by The General Organization of Cinema

A Woman's Confession (1971)
Nadia Lotfi
directed by Saad Arafa, produced by The General Organization of Cinema

The Airport Belle (1971)
Hassan Yousef and Naglaa Fathi
directed by el-Sayed Bedeir, produced by Abdel Rehim Abu Ouf Films

A Woman and A Man (1971)
Rushdi Abaza and Nahed Sherif
directed by Hossam-Eddine Mustafa, produced by Ihab el-Leithy Films and Hayman Film

The Diaries of Miss Manal (1971)
Nelly
directed by Abbas Kamel, produced by The General Organization of Cinema

The Forbidden Love (1971)
Madiha Yousri and Shukri Sarhan
directed by Hassan el-Imam, produced by Madiha Yousri Films

Some Live Twice (1971)
Ychia Chahine and Sanaa Gamil
directed by Kamal Attiya, produced by The General Organization of Cinema

Something on My Chest (1971)
Rushdi Abaza
directed by Kamal el-Sheikh, produced by Ramses Naguib

Daily Games (1971)
Taheya Carioca, Nabila Ebeid, Ezzat el-Alayli, and Said Saleh
directed by Khalil Shawki, produced by The General Organization of Cinema

Music, Spies, and Love (1971)

directed by Nour el-Demerdash, produced by The General Organization of Cinema

One in a Million (1971)
Thulathi Adwaa el-Masrah (Lights of the Theater Trio)
directed by Ashraf Fahmi, produced by Ittihad el-Fanniyin (Abdel Halim Nasr)

My Wife and the Dog (1971)
Soad Hosni and Mahmoud Morsi
directed by Said Marzouk, produced by The General Organization of Cinema

The Limelight (1972)
Nahed Yousri
directed by Hussein Helmi El-Mohandes (the Engineer), produced by The General Organization of Cinema

People and the Nile (1972)

directed by Yousef Chahine, produced by The General Organization of Cinema with Mosifilm (Moscow)

Zero Hour (1972)
Samia Gamal
directed by Hussein Helmi (El-Mohandes), produced by Mohsen Fergany

A Song at the Passage (1972)
Mahmoud Morsi, Mahmoud Yassin, Salah El-Saadani, and Ahmed Marei
directed by Ali Abdel Khalek, produced by The General Organization of Cinema and New Cinema Group

Forbidden Images (1972)

directed by Mohamed Abdel Aziz, Ashraf Fahmi, and Madkour Thabet, produced by The General Organization of Cinema

Story of a Girl Called Marmar (1972)
Soheir el-Morshidi and Salah Mansour
directed by Barakat, produced by The General Organization of Cinema

A Nose and Three Eyes (1972)
Salah Mansour and Naeema el-Soghayar
directed by Hussein Kamal, produced by Magda Films

El Sukkariyya (The Sugar Bowl) (1973)
Abdel Moneim Ibrahim and Hoda Sultan
directed by Hassan el-Imam, produced by El-Mutahida Cinema (Sobhi Farahat)

Estranged (1973)
Soad Hosni and Ezzat el-Alayli
directed by Saad Arafa, produced by Al-Tali'a Film Company

An Invitation to Life (1973)
Salah Zulficar and Mervat Amin
directed by Medhat Bakir, produced by The General Organization of Cinema

Night and Rails (1973)
Samira Ahmed
directed by Ashraf Fahmi, produced by The General Organization of Cinema

A Schoolgirl's Romance (1973)
Naglaa Fathi
directed by Helmi Halim, produced by The Arabic Film (Hala Helmi Halim)

The Beggar (1973)
Mahmoud Morsi and Nelly
directed by Hossam-Eddine Mustafa, produced by The General Organization of Cinema

254

Wild Flowers (1973)
Nadia Lotfi and Mohi Ismail
directed by Yousef Francis, produced by The General Organization of Cinema

The Backstairs (1973)
Hassan Yousef, Muwafak Bahgat, Kays Abdel Fattah, and Helmi Hilali
directed by Atef Salem, produced by The General Organization of Cinema

The Girls Must Get Married (1973)
Naglaa Fathi and Ahmed el-Sonbati
directed by Ali Reda, produced by Ali Reda and Co.

The Other Man (1973)
Salah Zulficar
directed by Mohamed Bassiouni, produced by The General Organization of Cinema

The Innocents (1974)
Mervat Amin and Ghassan Mattar
directed by Mohamed Rady, produced by Al-Tali'a Film Company

Wonderful Trip (1974)
Mohamed Awad
directed by Hassan el-Saifi, produced by El-Saifi Films

A Jungle of Legs (1974)
Mahmoud Yassin and Nelly
directed by Hossam-Eddine Mustafa, produced by Gina Film

A Woman in Love (1974)
Shadia
directed by Ashraf Fahmi, produced by Mohamed Ragaai

Bamba Kashar (1974)
Nadia el-Gindi and Emad Hamdi
directed by Hassan el-Imam, produced by Emad Hamdi Films

The Enmity of Brothers (1974)
Nour el-Sherif and Mervat Amin
directed by Hossam-Eddine Mustafa, produced by Gina Film

Amira My Love (1974)
Soheir el-Babli and Hussein Fahmi
directed by Hassan el-Imam, produced by Um Kalthoum Al-Hamidi Films

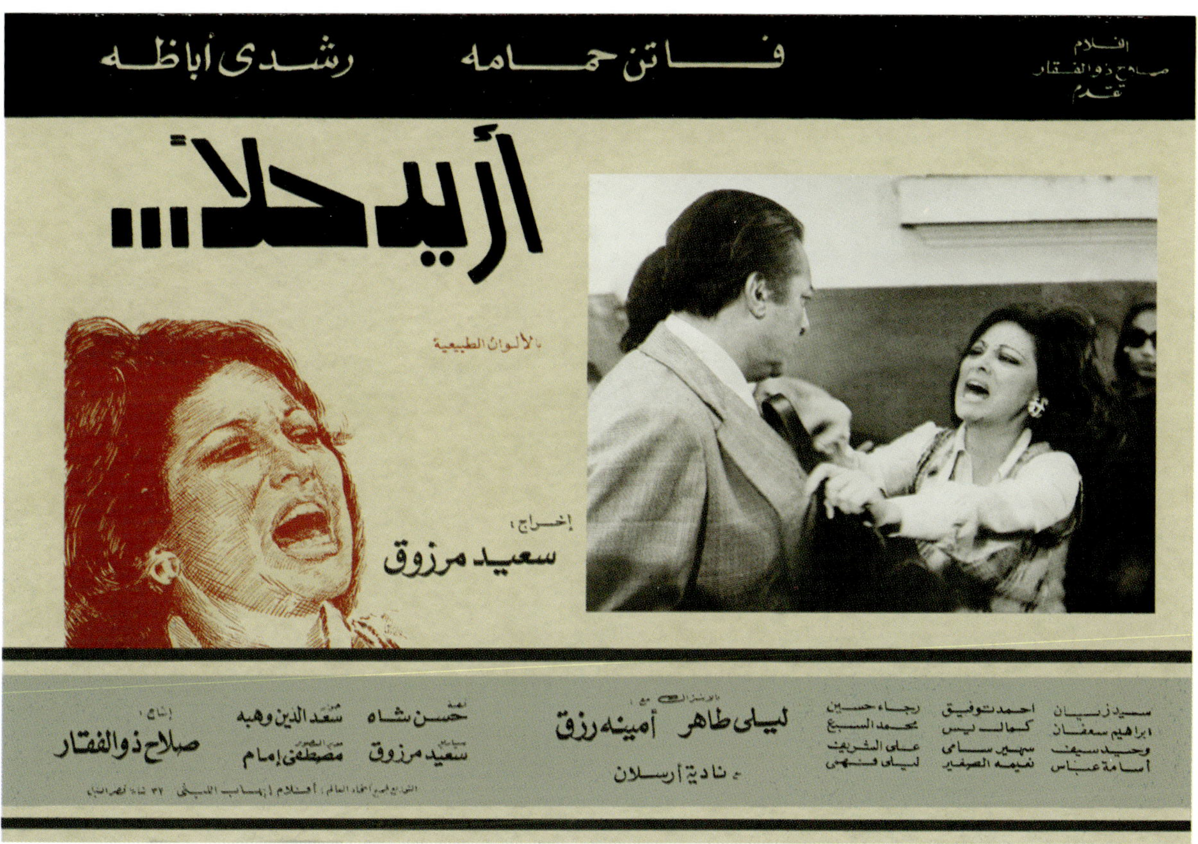

I Want a Solution (1975)
Faten Hamama and Rushdi Abaza
directed by Said Marzouk, produced by Salah Zulficar Films

On Cellophane Paper (1975)
Nadia Lotfi and Ahmed Mazhar
directed by Hussein Kamal, produced by Mohamed Ragaai

Sabreen (1975)
Naglaa Fathi
directed by Hossam-Eddine Mustafa, produced by Ittihad Films (Abbas Helmi)

The Siren (1975)
Ihab Nafea and Mervat Amin
directed by Hussein Kamal, produced by Magda Films

269

The Coward and Love (1975)
Shams el Baroudi
directed by Hassan Yousef, produced by Hassan Yousef Films

Melody in My Life (1975)
Farid el-Atrash and Mervat Amin
directed by Barakat, produced by El-Mutahida Cinema (Sobhi Farahat)

Life Is a Feast (1975)
Afaf Radi and Mahmoud Yassin
directed by Hussein Kamal, produced by Sout Al-Fann Films

Karnak (1975)
Soad Hosni
directed by Ali Badrakhan, produced by El-Leithy Film

Viva Zalata (1976)
Fuad el-Mohandes and Chewikar
directed by Hassan Hafez, produced by Fuad El-Mohandes Films

Convergence (1977)
Mahmoud Morsi and Habiba
directed by Sobhi Shafik, produced by The Cinema, Theater and Music Authority and Sobhi Shafik

Barefoot on a Golden Bridge (1977)
Mervat Amin and Shafik Galal
directed by Atef Salem, produced by Ittihad Films (Abbas Helmi)

Oh the Night and Time (1977)
Warda and Adel Adham
directed by Ali Reda, produced by Badie Sobhi Films

El-Aqmar (1978)
Nour el-Sherif, Mohi Ismail, and Said Saleh
produced and directed by Hisham Abul-Nasr

The Invisible Trick (1979)
Nagwa Fuad and Mahmoud el-Meligi
directed by Yehia el-Alami, produced by El-Masri Films (Askalani and Gamgoum)

El-Batniyya (1980)
Nadia el Gindi and Mahmoud Yassin
directed by Hossam-Eddine Mustafa, produced by Mohamed Mokhtar Films

A Warm Winter Night (1981)
Adel Imam and Yusra
directed by Ahmed Fuad, produced by F. N. Films

A Date for Dinner (1981)
Soad Hosni and Ahmed Zaki
directed by Mohamed Khan, produced by Al-Gawhara Films

Houseboat Nº 70 (1982)
Ahmed Zaki and Tayseer Fahmi
directed by Khairy Beshara, produced by Mima Cinema Production

Shame (1982)
Nour el-Sherif and Noura
directed by Ali Abdel Khalek, produced by Adwaa el-Cinema

283

The Bus Driver (1983)
Nour el-Sherif
directed by Atef el-Tayeb, produced by Hadirama

5 Doors (1983)
Nadia el-Gindi
directed by Nader Galal, produced by Mohamed Mokhtar Films

The Teacher and the Dancer (1983)
Nadia el-Gindi and Mahmoud Yassin
directed by Ahmed Yassin, produced by Al-Gawhara Films

The Dancer and the Drummer (1984)
Nabila Ebeid and Mohamed Reda
directed by Ashraf Fahmi, produced by Sima Film (Farouk Fathalla)

Streetplayer (1984)
Adel Imam
directed by Mohamed Khan, produced by El-Sohba Films

The Last Respectable Man (1984)
Nour el-Sherif and Boussy
directed by Samir Seif, produced by N. P. Film

Allah's World (1985)
Maali Zayed
directed by Hassan el-Imam, produced by Idea

Adieu Bonaparte (1985)

directed by Yousef Chahine, produced by Misr International Films

El-Kif (1985)
Mahmoud Abdel Aziz
directed by Ali Abdel Khalek, produced by Adwaa el-Cinema

The Collar and the Bracelet (1986)
Sherihan
directed by Khairy Beshara, produced by El-Alamiya TV and Cinema Company

The Beginning (1986)
Ahmed Zaki and Yusra
directed by Salah Abu Seif, produced by El-Alamiya TV and Cinema Company

294

The Sixth Day (1986)
Mohsen Mohi-Eddine
directed by Yousef Chahine, produced by Misr International Films

The Dwarves Are Coming (1986)
Yehia el-Fakharani and Gamil Ratib
directed by Sherif Arafa, produced by Osama Fawzi and Sherif Shaaban

The Dreams of Hind and Camilia (1988)
Naglaa Fathi and Mohamed Kamel
directed by Mohamed Khan, produced by El-Alamiya TV and Cinema Company (Hussein el-Kalla)

Bitter Day, Sweet Day (1988)
Faten Hamama
directed by Khairy Beshara, produced by El-Alamiya TV and Cinema Company (Hussein el-Kalla)

The Aragoz (1989)
Omar Sherif
directed by Hani Lasheen, produced by Gemini Cinema Production (Hani Lasheen and Mona Gabr)

The She-Devil That Loved Me (1990)
Mohamed Sobhi and Libliba
directed by Samir Seif, produced by Screen 2000 (Safwat Ghattas)

Egyptian Citizen (1991)
Omar Sharif
directed by Salah Abu Seif, produced by El-Alamiya TV and Cinema Company (Hussein el-Kalla)

Ice Cream in Gleem (1992)
Amr Diab and Simone
directed by Khairy Beshara, produced by Al-Ahram Cinema & Video (Ibrahim Shawki)

The Efreets of the Tarmac (1996)
Salwa Khattab
directed by Osama Fawzi, produced by Gerges Fawzi Films

Ismailia Back and Forth (1997)
Mohamed Fuad and Mohamed Heneidy
directed by Karim Diaa-Eddine, produced by El-Nasr Films (Mohamed Hassan Ramzi) and Hassan Ibrahim & Co.